Grouse Hunter's Guide

*Solid facts, insights,
and observations on
how to hunt the ruffed grouse*

Dennis Walrod

Stackpole Books

Published by
STACKPOLE BOOKS
Cameron and Kelker Streets
P.O. Box 1831
Harrisburg, PA 17105

Printed in the U.S.A.

Library of Congress Cataloging in Publication Data

Walrod, Dennis.
  Grouse hunter's guide.

  Includes index.
  1. Grouse shooting.   I. Title.
SK325.G7W35   1985   799.2'48616   85-8145
ISBN 0-8117-0772-5

This book is dedicated to the ruffed grouse that get away, the ones that do not fall when the gun is fired. These are the grouse which define the standards of sportsmanship, promising us an unforeseen ending for when, again, we return to the uplands in search of challenge.

Acknowledgments

Special thanks go to Ken Szabo of the Loyal Order of Dedicated Grouse Hunters for so generously providing the hunter research data that is presented in this book. The insights into *real* grouse hunterdom (gun, gauge, and dog preferences; covert ratings; and annual kills per season), gleaned from the logged data of several hundred dedicated LODGH members, have been immensely useful to my writing. If it were possible, I would invite every one of those contributors of grouse hunting wisdom and experience to share my favorite coverts. I want to express gratitude to Tom Martinson, freelance wildlife photographer, for the many excellent photographs of wild ruffed grouse that grace these pages. There is appreciation also to be expressed to the Ruffed Grouse Society for permission to borrow a paragraph here and there from articles of mine that had earlier appeared in *The Drummer*. And may I thank all the grouse researchers (notably Gordon Gullion and John Kris) for their contributions to our understanding of upland hunting's greatest gamebird.

Now we get close to home. Without the willing assistance of certain hunting partners (Rick Sanders, Bob Ungerer, Howard Roche, George Videll, and Stephen Hook), who were each deputized at various moments to stop in their tracks to either be photographed or to do the photographing, I wouldn't have been able to illustrate this book with the authentic actions of real grouse hunters. My wife, Peg, also clicked a shutter or two in the kitchen and somehow managed to type the complete manuscript for this book while maintaining order in the household. In various ways the rest of the family (Laura, Karin, Megan, Jennifer, and Nathan) also participated in the "field research" and the preparation of this book, although sometimes in ways that were not totally recognizable as being beneficial to the cause.

Contents

1

A Different Sort of Hunting Sport

The essence of grouse hunting, including the allure and the mystique, the beginning and the end, can be described in a scenario that often lasts less than five seconds.

First, the stage setting. You are amidst the tangled glories of an autumn covert where grouse are known to lurk. Something very special is about to happen; an unidentified instinct tightens your grip on the gun. Even though a myriad of interesting brushpiles, pricker bushes, grape vine festooneries, and other grouse haunts have just recently been passed without incident, this next place seems different. Maybe the songbirds are suddenly quiet, a cloud's edge may have crossed the sun, or perhaps the dog has assumed a stiffened gait and a slowing of speed. The ground under your feet seems to lose stability, as though your next step might trigger a trembling that would alarm the woodlands and shake you into awkwardness. The gift of total awareness begins to glow from within as though a rheostat had

been twisted to full ON. The reality of the present instant becomes
starkly intense. We are talking magic here. There is clarity and purpose now, replacing autumnal daydreams. Another step is taken and
then another; your body is not listening to your mind. Then it happens. Thunder erupts, a sound so wild, so thrilling, that the human
heart swells to embrace it. A ruffed grouse is in the air, blurred wings
clawing against the sky for more air, more speed. Seldom are you
privileged to know the exact spot from which it sprang, this phantom,
this grouse, this elusive target. The gun, a featherlight only moments
ago, becomes heavy and slow to move. Time also slows down. Your
mind will record what happens next with great clarity while your
body protests that there's *not time enough!* to swing the gun accurately
and purposefully along the path that the grouse is slashing and tearing against the backdrop of an autumn sky. But somehow, hunter's
reflexes take control, overriding thought, and the gun's muzzle is
made to transcribe a neat, quick arc that first follows and then catches
up with that source of thunder. The gun fires new lightning. There is
shock, a momentary glimpse of wings suddenly folded, and then a
plummeting. Elation surges. Then sadness flickers, but doesn't stay in
focus long enough to be reconciled. A ruffed grouse has been
downed.

In the mind's eye, the world resumes turning, clouds commence
drifting, and the moment of expectant stillness from which brief violence sprang is over, once again. You will remember the event, as all
grouse hunters do, for a very long time. Every grouse flush is different
from all others. We might, along the way, permit some of our misses
to fade from memory, but successful hits are always there for recall.
And so will be that strange feeling, remembered now, that you positively knew something was about to happen.

Several brushworn grouse hunting buddies and acquaintances
have, over the years, spoken to me about a "feeling of expectation," a
sense of great certainty that often precedes their observation of a
ruffed grouse suddenly in flight. These hunters were, one and all,
embarrassed to reveal this "feeling," as though they were confessing a
hidden belief in flying saucers. I understand their embarrassment:
one does not comfortably mix metaphysics with natural science.

There have also been times when the "feeling" has come upon
me, and yet no grouse has flushed, nary a one. I have, on these occasions, accused myself of playing mental games under the guise of
wishful thinking. No other creature I have hunted uses the element of
surprise to such a highly developed extent. One, maybe two seconds
pass and the bird is gone; the woodlands are again silent.

Ruffed grouse use the element of surprise as an escape tactic. The sudden flush on powerful wings and the quick turns made possible by the broad fantail make for an almost unbelievable airborne performance. *Photo by T. Martinson.*

I have taken non-hunters into the woods, people who would never have ventured there otherwise, and we have occasionally flushed grouse. My eyes would automatically observe much detail of a flight, the bird's direction, sometimes even the glitter of its frantic eye and the color phase of the feathers. My neophyte partners might then exclaim something like "What made that sound?" or "What? I didn't hear or see a *thing*!"

It's easy to understand why the explosively quick flush of the ruffed grouse has reached almost legendary proportions; perhaps herein lies a hint of explanation for the grouse hunter's sense of an impending flush, that special déjà vu of recognition. Simply stated, it goes like this: A grouse flushes so fast, is gone so quickly, that the mind just can't believe what it saw. But the brain insists that there must be a logic, a beginning and an end to every event it observes. Body chemistries rush to fill in the gaps, to mount the gun, to identify and safely shoot. The sudden, total reality of a grouse is often more than our senses can easily handle.

To act in a knowing manner, we (rationalizing) . . . we must have known it would happen. That's right! our hunter's mind tells us, we *did* know that grouse would flush! And so, possibly, this is why grouse hunters admit to one another—here and there at social gatherings or around the fireside, always out of earshot of others who neither know nor care to know the mysteries of grouse hunting—that we sometimes get this strange "feeling" about grouse. What we don't admit, even to ourselves, is that we have literally talked ourselves into believing it, this trick of our senses.

I would prefer to believe, and so would you, that there is a magic contained in grouse hunting that transcends a short-lived confusion of the nervous system. Yes, I think I'll stick with the magic, a touch of it here and there. There is a certain bittersweet haunting that seems to possess my favorite coverts, especially towards sundown when lengthening shadows begin to creep through abandoned orchards, spilling over stone fences and filling the outlines of deserted foundations of houses where countryfolk from a bygone era once farmed. Don't listen too keenly, too late past sundown, or you might hear their voices.

A grouse hunter, always expecting the unexpected, is naturally alert to and ever-perceiving of the surrounding woodlands. Does this make the grouse hunter a better sort of person? Or, just possibly, are only certain types of people drawn to this better sort of sport? I don't know. But, I'll claim this much: I've never met a grouse hunter who wasn't a true sportsman of the finest kind—and every one of them has had an overactive imagination.

The Flush Is the Goal

Ask a grouse hunter how his luck ran during a day in the coverts, and you'll likely get a curious reply. Almost any representative of the brushworn leagues will first tell you how many grouse he flushed, and whether most of these were within shotgun range or not. Then, if you appear to be an attentive and interested listener, odds are good that you will next be told the number of shots that were fired.

Just because a grouse flushes doesn't mean that an honest opportunity to take a sporting shot has been offered. Over the long haul, the average hunter only shoots at about a third of the grouse he flushes. Grouse are quick! So, now we get down to the nitty-gritty, the bottom line: the body count. Lips quivering with anticipation, we ask "Well—uh—how many grouse did you kill?" A look of unshaded contempt will cross the brushworn hunter's eyes. This question of the kill is perhaps not totally irrelevant to the success of a grouse hunt, but it is a query of a personal nature. It's sort of like asking someone what their checkbook balance is. Interesting, sure, but none of our business either.

As when any crass question is posed, we probably won't get a direct answer. Our grouse hunter, eyes now squinted in the direction of a possible escape from our penetrating question, will reply with either a vague comment or an outright lie. "Didn't get as many of 'em as I should've" is a typically evasive reply. "Got my limit" is usually a falsehood, that is, unless our reluctant interviewee is one of those admirable fellows who sets a personal bag limit considerably lower than the legal daily limit. Regardless, we seldom will be told exactly how many (if any) grouse a hunter has killed.

There are exceptions, of course, but only one or two. If our grouse hunter has just scored a double, dropping two grouse that flushed simultaneously—a very rare happening—we will be told every detail of the incident. The story will take at least half an hour in the telling, even though the act itself lasted only two heartbeats and one deep breath. In fact, getting rid of a grouse-doubles storyteller can be a real problem. He sometimes brings his own bourbon and camps himself by your fireside until even your spouse, children, and dogs have heard the story nineteen times.

Early one October morning, a hunting buddy of mine, a seasoned veteran of the upland coverts, killed three grouse with two shots. *Bang! bang! thud, thud . . . thud!!* By midafternoon he had telephoned *everyone* he knew. By nightfall he was into the sauce pretty heavily, and some of us began wishing he'd never gone grouse hunting in the first place.

The aftermath of a celebration of remarkable grouse hunting luck can be a very sobering period of reflection. With hindsight, luck is seen to be a rare currency that shouldn't be spent all in one place. The grouse hunter knows that he will have to pay dearly for a momentary burst of good fortune in the grouse coverts. Yes, a weighty heft to the gamebag nearly always means that the next dozen grouse will be free to thunder away unscathed. Maybe even two dozen, with nary a feather afloat. The grouse hunter who is reluctant to talk about his successes is probably hoping that Lady Luck won't discover his secret and then try to balance the scales. We take our chances; we pay our dues. If not now, then later for certain.

Flush rates remain as our best means of communicating the success of a grouse hunt. You can't really share the basic experience—the ripe tang of the autumn air, the playing of poplar shadows when a breeze moves, or the way Pup's wagging tail stiffens with a quiver when her point becomes suddenly solid. You also can't count dead birds if you didn't get any. Does no kill mean no fun? Of course not.

Experienced ruffed grouse hunters define the quality of a hunt (when such definitions are needed) with a set of three numbers, such as 7-3-1. These particular numbers mean that seven grouse were flushed, three were shot at, and one was bagged. Very often that last number is a zero; but if the first number is a big one, it will be announced with a proud smile.

All grouse hunting strategies are based on making grouse flush skyward, within shotgun range, so that a decent, sporting shot can be taken. Literally, you can't shoot 'em if you can't see 'em. And rarely will you see a grouse until it has been flushed. Hunting the coverts in a manner and method that causes grouse to flush close by is the most important fundamental of this very special sport. If a hunter can't reliably do this, then discouragement will be the only predictable result. Most other hunting sports—whether the game is deer or squirrels, mourning doves or waterfowl—involve tactics that place the hunter where the game is likely to later appear of its own free will. Call it what you want; this method is best described as ambushing. Maybe even bushwacking.

The ruffed grouse hunter, by contrast, works hard for his game. He wades deep into the tangled coverts to tickle the proximity fuses held within the breast of every grouse. A yard of distance can mean the difference between continued silence and a sudden burst of winged thunder. A knowledge of both grouse and habitat behavior is essential, whether the hunter goes afield alone or in the company of a bird dog.

The flush itself becomes the grouse hunter's primary goal, and thereby the sport's chief measure of success. Because of this, the ruffed grouse should only be shot from full flight. There's no written law that ruffed grouse can't be shot on the ground or out of their evening perches. To do so is not technically illegal, but such actions border on the profane, if not the immoral. If it's meat you're after, save time and effort by going to the supermarket. For pure sport, depend only on your learned ability to flush grouse, hitting or missing them then being a measure of your shooting, rather than hunting, skills.

The Average Grouse Hunter's Performance

Asking another grouse hunter how he performed during the past season is not a very polite thing to do. Ruffed grouse hunting is a different sort of sport, with emphasis placed more upon quality than quantity—and personal standards of quality are different for each of us. Still, the nagging question persists.

The ruffed grouse is an elusive bird, sometimes difficult to find and always difficult to center in a shot pattern. Grouse explode into flight at the most unexpected times; they dodge and dart away through the foliage with uncanny flying skill; and they're usually gone from sight within two very brief seconds. In strict terms of hit-and-miss, the average grouse hunter could be classified as a failure the majority of the time. Perhaps this is why we have this all-pervading curiosity about each other's performance in the grouse coverts.

The grouse hunter who has just missed half a dozen or so grouse, including some of the easiest shots ever offered to mankind, is not exactly suffering physical pain—but he's not very happy either. It would be of no small solace for said hunter to discover that the frequent missing of ruffed grouse is more the rule than the exception. Many surveys have been conducted by state game agencies and special-interest conservation groups to determine grouse hunter success rates. Every single one of them (to my knowledge) has shown that the ruffed grouse is the most difficult gamebird to bag in America.

I have been particularly interested in the results of surveys conducted by Ken Szabo, publisher of *Grouse Tales*, which is the official publication of the Loyal Order of Dedicated Grouse Hunters. LODGH statistics are based upon the experiences of people sufficiently devoted to the sport to call themselves grouse hunters and to fork up $7.50 per year for the bimonthly newsletter. (Address is: *Grouse Tales*, 17130 Chatfield, Cleveland, Ohio 44111.)

The upland hunter works hard for the occasional grouse that falls before the gun. Many hunters personally score a flush almost as high as a bird in the hand.

When you read the following statistics supplied by the Loyal Order, you're seeing the essence of grouse hunting success rates, not the results of state surveys which include anyone who happened to take a pot shot at a booming grouse while on his way into the squirrel hardwoods. Surprisingly, perhaps, the data shows that even experienced grouse hunters would be hungry fellows indeed if they had to rely on their seasonal bags for sustenance.

Results of 1982–1983 Grouse Season
(258 respondents from five major grouse hunting states)

Total hours hunted	61.5
Total flushes	95.5
Average flushes per hour	1.55
Total number of grouse shot at	30.4
Average percent of flushes shot at	33.6%
Average percent of shots that killed grouse	33.8%
Average number of grouse killed per hunter	10.2

In a sentence, dedicated grouse hunters flushed about 96 grouse, shot at about a third of the grouse that flushed, and bagged only about one bird for every three shots fired. This means that the *average* number of grouse killed per hunter was 10.2.

But hold on just a minute! The word *average* does not mean all that it might imply. If you shoot broadside at a lion and graze first the tip of his nose and again the tip of his rump, does this mean that *on the average* you hit the heart? No, of course not. The *typical* Loyal Order grouse hunter, however, actually bags only about five grouse a year (as is explained in more detail in chapter 10). Here's a clue: Include just one millionaire in a survey of low-income families, and the data will indicate that everyone has plenty of disposable income. Aha! It's the same with grouse hunter surveys. There are a few hunters out there in the autumn coverts who are superb wingshots, members of a true elite in terms of skill, but representing only a miniscule fraction of the grouse hunting fraternity. These few bias the average, making the rest of us look like bumbling clods.

So, where are we now, having had our dark questions about grouse hunter success answered in black and white? Nowhere, really. If a comparison of oneself with other grouse hunters is personally necessary, then consider whether the sport itself gains or suffers from such a comparison. Let's resolve to go into the ripe autumn coverts in search not of pounds of flesh, but of quality—in a hunting sport that is so wonderfully resistant to our best efforts that we can bang away at it, with every ounce of skill and perseverance we possess, without the fear of tipping the scales too far in the direction of excess. Let's set our own standards and have fun trying to achieve them. A fallen grouse should represent far more than a point scored in some silly game played without compassion.

A Viewpoint (The Author's Credentials)

Please understand that the writer of this book is a rather mediocre wingshot, the type of person who abuses a shotgun by ignoring scratches in the wood and corrosion in the barrel, and who is at least two months overdue so far this year on his training program for the youngest dog. These are poor credentials for a grouse hunter. I also have never shot a double in grouse, and the memories of past opportunities to achieve such a feat are beads of sweat upon my brow that never dry.

Yet, for all these failings, I am still one very skilled grouse-finder. Place me in a vehicle on a cross-country highway, and I will detect out of the corner of my eye, at fifty-five miles per hour, where grouse can be found. I make that claim. I know that grouse are plentiful in the woodlands, maybe even as abundant as robins in a parkland—but better hidden. The key to the secret of finding grouse is, simply put, to get into the right habitat and *look for them*!

I had a trapline during my early teenage years, and ruffed grouse were (to me) those noisy birds that kept surprising me every time I passed through certain types of habitat. Occasionally I hunted them with a single-shot shotgun and managed to scare some of the birds as much as they had scared me. My reading of stories about African safaris and out-West hunting ventures led me to relegate grouse hunting to the ranks of the commonplace. Grouse hunting was something you did when you couldn't travel to exotic locations. Shooting rats at the town dump (back when such things were allowed) offered as much sporting shooting as did grouse hunting, at least as far as I was concerned.

Don't misunderstand; I did not feel a contempt for the ruffed grouse. No, not by any stretch of the imagination. What I was thinking back in those days was that if a fellow was planning to seriously take up the sport of hunting, he should consider only game that was *difficult* to find and *easy* to shoot. After all, I was seeing grouse nearly every time I looked for them. Not much sport in that! The fact that I was missing every single grouse I shot at seemed irrelevant in those early days.

Even now, I still dream of going on an African safari. But my perspective on the elements of sport and fair chase has undergone an about-face, and for nearly three decades I have been able to march into the autumn domain of the ruffed grouse believing that grouse hunting is one of the highest forms of sport hunting. My attitude immediately altered course in this direction when the first grouse dropped in front of my pointed, fired gun. I got him! It was that quick. The grouse had flushed from the undergrowth of a hawthorn thicket; I had whirled around towards the sound into the setting sun, had seen the bird rising, and had fired before the gun even touched to my shoulder. The bird dropped to the ground and thundered there for a moment, wings beating fiercely until it died seconds later. In the ensuing silence, I realized, as though through revelation, how many dozens upon dozens of grouse I had missed before this first bird was finally claimed. Hefting the bird and admiring close-up the patterns of its feathered colorations, I knew right then that trophies come in many forms—and that ruffed grouse is definitely one of them. Any creature that difficult to kill was obviously on a par with Cape buffalo and spotted leopards as a world-class prize of the hunting game.

As a veteran grouse hunter, I now realize that success in drawing blood is not essential to my sense of fulfillment. A hunter's luck ebbs and tides, and shouldn't really be important enough at any given moment to use as sole criterion for judging the value of an afternoon's hunt. You lose some; you win some. It's when you start winning (or losing) all the time that sport ceases and scoring begins. I believe that the greatest single attraction of grouse hunting is that you can throw body and soul into it, and yet the brick wall of uncertainty (which the *next* flushed bird presents) will protect you from unwanted, excessive success. Shoot three grouse in a row and the fourth bird will almost invariably rescue you from becoming a game hog.

Inner Standards of Excellence

Grouse hunting isn't easy. You couldn't afford to pay a person enough these days to go out and make a living gunning grouse for the table. Certainly not at prevailing prices for chicken flesh. I'm not going to try to tell you that grouse hunters are masochists. No, not at all. Actually, those of us who go plodding through tangled briars and thorny covers in search of ruffed grouse are seeking neither punishment nor meat-on-the-table. We are instead searching for the furthest edge of civilization, the outer rim from which we can look back and perhaps see ourselves and our everyday world with greater clarity.

We neither pit ourselves against dangerous game nor strain the limits of common sense in our endeavors. Sure, we might be aptly classified as thrill-seekers, but only if you count the flavor of a wild apple plucked from a century-old orchard as one possible thrill. Or the solid point of a good bird dog as another one. We are thrilled by the sights and sounds and smells of autumn woodlands, and we become positively euphoric when a new covert is discovered, full of grouse and tomorrow's promise. When a grouse rockets skyward, boosted forth by our having unlocked the secrets of both habitat and strategy, pure joy reigns supreme.

A true grouse hunter understands that spilled blood is not a criterion of success in this very special hunting sport. If by some tweak of environmental fate the ruffed grouse population should suddenly explode until there were more grouse than robins and starlings combined, we would surely see a reverse trend in the number of grouse hunters afield. Expressing great disgust at such a turn of events, the small select army of brushworn grouse hunters would turn on their

The ruffed grouse is upland hunting's worthiest trophy, a silent shadow one moment and violent thunder an instant later. *Photo by T. Martinson.*

heels in search of more demanding sport, such as dry-fly trout fishing or hunting the wild turkey with bow and arrow. You can't chugalug a fine wine and still appreciate its subtler qualities. Many grouse hunters envy the catch-and-release option that is given to anglers and would be glad to toss a fallen grouse back to the sky if it could some- how burst into renewed flight at this moment of freedom.

This is not solely my opinion; I've heard it expressed many times and in various versions by other ruffed grouse hunters. I know one fellow who traveled deep into Canada where the grouse are so toler- ant of a human's close approach that they can be killed with a stick. This fellow devised several means of getting the birds to flush so that he could take shots that were at least remotely sporting. Before long, however, he had dug out his rod and reel and gone fishing, seeking sport that exceeded his capacity for guaranteed success.

The grouse hunter, the sort of person who doesn't shave his golf score and yet who might phone in an alleged illness to steal an Octo- ber day away from a forty-hour workweek, is a person whose ethics are based more upon quality than quantity. He or she judges success in terms of grouse flushed rather than in grouse bagged.

Each grouse hunter sets his or her own personal standards of excellence. Some, because they cannot relax and truly enjoy the hunt until they have killed the first, the tenth, or even the hundredth bird, have temporarily lost sight of those elements of grouse hunting which attracted them to the sport in the first place. All the rest, the hunters who take their shots when and as circumstances offer them but do not harshly question the technical reasons for their frequent misses, are the lucky ones. Each bagged bird becomes an unexpected treat, pro- viding just enough impetus to step into the next covert with all enthu- siasm intact and functioning.

The Species is Holy—But One Grouse Isn't

We like to kill grouse. Now . . . isn't that a strange thing to say? In print, those words seem to convey a certain ruthlessness, a disdain for wildlife. And yet we truly care for our noble quarry. At the instant of the kill, the hunter and the gun and the grouse combine to become one. Form follows function, and during that brief moment of intercon- nected violence, it seems impossible that we might ever have missed the target. The cycle of planning, hunting, finding, and gathering-in is completed and started over when a grouse plummets to earth, and we sense a feeling of renewal.

The grouse, of course, dies, and there's the rub, the dark question mark that causes us to ask whether we really have a moral right to hunt the ruffed grouse with intent to kill. We stand holding the limp form of a ruffed grouse in hand, pondering (as we always do) the perfection in the feathered patterns, and wish however momentarily that a quick toss upward could restore the now-quieted thunder. But then pride of achievement takes ahold of us. The ruffed grouse is a worthy gamebird, and it's not really all that often that we get to hold one, to possess it and to know that our skills afield have shown a tangible payoff.

Most bag limits imposed by the various game agencies are something of a joke. Generally, state limits are set at three, four, or five grouse for one day's hunting. Anyone who has hunted grouse for longer than his first season knows that he is lucky if so much as a single grouse has been bagged by the end of a day afield. In ruffed grouse hunting, modern bag limits are less a restriction than they are an unattainable *goal*. In my home state of New York, approximately half the grouse hunters struggle for an entire season, attempting to bag what is actually one day's limit: four grouse!

There is certainly not a great need for self-restraint in this matter of killing grouse; the sport itself imposes sufficient controls. In fact, the complete removal of bag-limit restrictions would probably have negligible effect on the total yearly take. That's right; let ruffed grouse hunters shoot all the birds they could and you still wouldn't see any real decrease in next year's crop. After all, we're doing the best we can *now*—and all we can manage is a bird or two every once in a while. Sure, a very small percentage of grouse hunters, individuals whom the red gods have provided the combined gifts of shooting skill and ample leisure time, are able to bag fifty or a hundred grouse in a season's time. Would these people shoot even more grouse if the bag-limit restrictions were removed? No, I don't think so, at least not to the extent that the extra gunning would ruin the sport for the rest of us. The principle of diminishing returns would come into play, slowing down the blood-letting by making grouse more and more difficult to find within any given area that's being hunted by one of the super-gunners. Those who tend to measure their particular concept of the sport in terms of quantity (lots of grouse and fast gunning) will either depart for distant coverts or give the sport up entirely. A basic appeal of grouse hunting is that it is a sport not easy to be good at, one which tends to shed itself of those hunters who are somewhat less than sincere about the sporting aspects of fair chase.

It is, of course, technically possible for heavy hunting pressure to result in the destruction of all grouse within a single small covert, but only for one year. There would be new grouse the following year as a result of the autumn dispersal of young flocks from adjacent coverts. Still, even this good news is somewhat beside the point. The plain fact is that hunters aren't going to waste their precious hours afield trudging through a covert, attempting to shoot the last few hard-to-find grouse. They will hunt elsewhere, leaving a seed population of grouse to produce next year's crop.

The ruffed grouse is celebrated in many forms, such as wildlife art and outdoor literature; and it is revered by many people, including environmental action and special-interest conservation groups. Perhaps its most important patron is the individual upland hunter, who senses that a special magic can be found from hunting a quarry which escapes his best efforts often enough to seem to possess a touch of immortality. As a gamebird, the ruffed grouse has the distinction of being first class. But a hawk doesn't know this and wouldn't care if it did. From the window by my desk where I now write, I have often seen a red-tailed hawk spring from its perch in a honey locust to glide swiftly down through a covert of poplars that parallels the distant fenceline. The barn hides from me what happens next, but I always cringe reflexively and possessively when the hawk begins its predacious swoop. You see, those are *my* grouse down there in the woods past the hayfield. I want them preserved, saved whole and healthy for use in training my bird dogs and for possible photographic opportunities.

But Nature doesn't work that way. She takes what is needed, and any surplus is first to go. First come, first served. The ruffed grouse that meets its destiny as a gourmet supper is one less raw flesh meal for a hungry hawk or other predator.

The grouse hunter is one of the weights on Nature's balance, and a very insignificant one at that. Yes, we can go into the autumn coverts to hunt the ruffed grouse without feeling guilty if we happen to kill one or two or even the seemingly impossible "bag limit" goal. The ruffed grouse species can be revered as holy, but a day's bag is not sacred; it's a bonus for our dedication. A single fallen grouse can be appreciated for what it is without our feeling that we've damaged the holistic structure of the universe of the hunt. Let's care a little more about habitat, somewhat less about the solitary fallen bird.

The Four Ways to Hunt Ruffed Grouse

Ruffed grouse hunting is more highly stylized than are most of the hunting sports. There's a right way and a wrong way; for example, no self-respecting bird hunter would shoot a grouse while it's still lurking in ground cover. Yet, that selfsame hunter could, during another season, stalk a wild autumn turkey (a bird of a different feather) to the edge of a cornfield and then drop it before the huge fowl even had a chance to spread wings. That would be totally acceptable, and there would be heard no alarms ringing, no howling protests of unsportsmanlike conduct. So, why the inconsistency? Style. Also ritual, well-salted with tradition. You hunt grouse this way, not that way because . . . well, it's not considered sporting the other way.

Ironically, there has been a certain vagueness in much of the literature on grouse hunting. Somehow, the aura of mystique that surrounds the sport has inspired more detailed descriptions of the colors of the autumn leaves than of the practical side of how to hunt the bird. This is fine if you already know all there is to know about grouse hunting; but if you want to know the specifics of how to flush an extra grouse or two, the aesthetics of it all can seem to be somewhat beside the point. Understand that grouse hunters (and writers) not only tend to be biased as to *which* way grouse should be hunted, but we are also a little warped when it comes right down to the nitty-gritty of whether the *other* guy is doing things the right way.

I had hunted one particularly choice covert a few times each season for nearly a decade and had never seen another hunter in it, when one October day I was dismayed to find unwanted company. This other fellow was accompanied by two dogs: an English setter and a Labrador retriever. From afar I watched as he handled the dogs down through my favorite territory, the setter ranging on ahead while the Lab plodded along obediently at heel, waiting for the rare opportunity to retrieve whatever circumstances might provide. Hey, this guy had style!

Later, at roadside, I approached him to make conversation, hoping to learn in an unobtrusive manner (which is *my* style) whether he planned to come back again. Yes was the answer; he had hunted there several times and was pleased with the covert. On that particular day I had left my own bird dog at home, and it soon became obvious to me that the other hunter had classified me somewhere between Clod and Classless in his own hierarchy of grouse hunters. No dog, no sport. I could read it in his face. Feeling no need to apologize for doglessness, I even let the man give me an unneeded lecture on the reasons for keeping this covert a secret, and for not taking more than a responsible number of grouse from it.

Sure, I could now—right here in print—accuse this stranger of being a jerk and a snob, but I'm not going to do that. He had style.

Any hunter who has the patience and dedication to train two different breeds of dogs to behave in proper fashion in a grouse covert, both at the same time, is someone who comprehends the full meaning of the sportsmanship of fair chase. After all, what right have I to judge this man's concept of sportsmanship unless I hunt with at least *three* well-trained dogs afield!

I know another grouse hunter, a dedicated soul, who does all his bird shooting through a snub-nosed shotgun deerslug barrel and without benefit of a bird dog. No class? Nonsense. This fellow is a true sportsman and an accomplished grouse hunter in every sense of the word. He knows habitat, has flushing skills, and possesses a poetic understanding of conservation. If he could afford a good dog, he'd probably spend the money on a prettier shotgun. In conversation, this fellow has expressed the opinion several times that I perhaps have undue advantage because I usually hunt with a dog. Unfair, he claims; maybe even unsporting. Any dog can find a grouse, he says, but only a true sportsman can perform that function by himself.

So we are left with controversy, skilled grouse hunters arguing gently among themselves as to who has the true claim to fame, the authentic act that's hard to follow in terms of sheer style.

Remember, we're not talking here about bag limits or body counts or pounds of flesh. On any given day, certain styles of hunting work better than others, but this fact is thought by most of us to be irrelevant. Is the best artist the one who can paint the most pictures in a year's time? No, and neither should the various methods of grouse hunting be judged by the comparative numbers of birds brought to bag. Really, they all work, and they're fun.

The following four ways to hunt grouse are briefly described only to make the point that there are more ways than one to partake of grouse hunting and still maintain an authentic style. I am also motivated by the desire to assign to each of them a certain validity, even though there are single-minded purists among us who claim that there is only one way to hunt ruffed grouse—and it's their way.

1. *Alone, stalking habitat and using proximity to flush grouse* This method is grouse hunting in its purest and least complex form. A dog is not used. The hunter applies his own knowledge of grouse habitat to locate likely coverts, and then slowly walks, gun ready, towards each bit of cover where grouse might lurk. The lone grouse hunter is particularly aware of the existence of grapevines, hawthorns, poplars, edges along evergreens, and brushy fence corners. He hesitates near each objective, knowing that such actions are often required to trigger a flush.

There is a peculiar tension in this form of hunting because it is solely the proximity of the hunter that makes the game take to the air. If the hunter is off course by even a yard, a certain intimacy with nature is lost. His style of covering the covert will determine whether there will be a quantity of shots offered, or none at all. Any successes that are gained need be shared with no one.

2. With other hunters, each following a parallel or convergent course through a covert with intent to flush grouse towards each other This is the social form of grouse hunting, and it usually works only when each individual stays his course and keeps abreast of the other hunters. The major advantage of this method is that any grouse, once flushed, is potentially vulnerable to more than one gunner. A shout of "Mark left!" or "Mark right!" announces the sight of a bird suddenly aloft, and all guns go immediately on alert. Often, the hunter who flushes a grouse can't get off a safe shot because of the nearness of his partners. By the time a grouse passes the second or third hunter, its airspeed will be awesomely fast, and top shooting skills are required.

Another drawback to group hunting is that the individual hunter must often waste time walking through the wrong type of cover in order to fulfill his obligations to the other hunters. Still, group hunting is a good way for novices to learn by experience just where grouse are most apt to be found. If you ask a group hunter how well he did, he will reply that *we* flushed this or that many grouse and that *we* fired a certain number of shots.

3. With a bird dog that ranges outside shotgun range, locating and pointing grouse for the hunter to flush and (hopefully) shoot Hunting grouse with one of the pointing breeds is the classic form of the sport. Yet, many skilled grouse hunters have never even seen a trained bird dog, let alone hunted over one that could mesmerize a grouse into temporary immobility. English setters and English pointers are the traditional breeds, but Continental breeds, particularly the Brittany, are well represented in the upland coverts.

There is more hunter skill involved in hunting with a pointing dog than meets the eye. The dog must be handled in such a way, whether by hand signal or voiced or whistled commands, that it travels through the right kinds of cover. (An experienced dog that recognizes birdy cover and heads straight for it with total disregard for the hunter is just a few weekends away from becoming a worthless runaway.) A

One of the author's bird dogs, an English pointer named Kate, retrieves a fallen grouse.

proper grouse dog will keep checking back with the hunter's progress through a covert, and if the hunter makes the mistake of hunting poor cover, the dog will receive more than a fair share of the blame. On the other hand, a skilled grouse hunter can help an inexperienced dog learn the ropes of finding and holding grouse. It is the interaction between man and dog that makes this form of grouse hunting particularly enjoyable, and the wily ruffed grouse is the catalyst that gives the combined endeavor a worthy meaning.

You may think it's easy to shoot a grouse if a dog already has betrayed the bird's location, but it isn't. The pent-up tensions of the pointing scenario usually mess up a hunter's instinctive reflexes when a grouse finally flushes. Consequently, grouse hunters who take pointing breeds afield assign each "productive point" a value nearly as high as that of a bird in the gamebag.

4. With a flushing dog that ranges close to the gunner, locating and flushing grouse within shotgun range There once was a day when any dog that flushed a grouse on purpose was considered an ill-mannered scoundrel. That was before the springer spaniel and the Labrador retriever gained recognition in America for their utilitarian value as producers of upland game. Even close-ranging beagles, cocker spaniels, and various mongrels have been pressed into service. As a younger fellow, I hunted for several years with a dachshund mongrel. It pushed grouse out from under thick tangles that larger dogs might have avoided entirely.

A flushing dog is worthless if it won't stay close to the hunter. This method of hunting demands that the hunter be able to read the actions of his dog, that he be alert to an altered posture or position of the dog's tail so that a flush can be anticipated. Obviously, if the hunter doesn't place a close-ranging dog in the right kind of habitat, neither one of them will get to see any grouse. The flushing dog works best as an extra set of legs only with a hunter who knows what he's doing.

2

Ruffed Grouse—
King of Gamebirds

The flush of a ruffed grouse has been described with every possible verb that conveys the bird's sudden release of energy. Grouse explode, thunder, rocket, bolt, tear, rip, launch, catapult, hurtle, and detonate. No one ever says or writes, "The grouse flew away rapidly." To do so would be a ridiculous understatement. Grouse "leave" all right, and they do it "rapidly," but this sort of literal truth misses the point. Sometimes you have to exaggerate for the sake of accuracy. Grouse hunting is an emotional sort of thing. The facts-of-the-matter are often difficult to touch and feel.

I was hunting one cold winter day with one of my offspring in tow, when something happened that put the very essence of grouse hunting in sharp focus. My daughter Laura accidentally stepped on the frozen ice of a forest puddle. The echoing sound it made was like that of a grouse splitting the cold air with sharp wingbeats. For one brief instant, I thought it *was* a grouse. The muscles of my arms twitched as my hunter's instincts responded to a call for action. Twitch is all they did; the gun didn't move. I smiled to myself and kept walking. But the adrenaline flowed anyway, unstoppered by the reality of no bird, no flush. A second or two later, my heart raced, my throat swelled with the rush of blood, and I had to stop and take a few deep breaths to settle down. Grouse! It had all been a fiction, yet I had been a momentary believer. I had been thrilled by a phantom.

I wondered: Do I also react this way when a real grouse flushes? I think the answer is yes. There is probably the same rush of emotion, but the intense flurry of activity involved in trying to shoot at the bird absorbs the feeling and then uses it. Other species of gamebirds are fun to hunt, interesting in their habits, and often a challenge to the hunter. But they're not capable of *shocking* the way a ruffed grouse is. Ducks glide quietly into decoys or spring into near-silent, straightaway flight. Pheasants cackle wickedly at the crest of their sudden jump into flight, but then spend too much time leveling off in their getaway attempt. Woodcock titter on soft, feathered wings. These birds are always a surprise, but they're more a gunner's living target than a challenge to the human nervous system. Even the initial intensity of a quail covey flush is too quickly dispersed as the little birds fly off in their separate directions.

Only the ruffed grouse combines all the elements of speed, surprise, evasiveness, and intimidation that other gamebirds use, by comparison, only in moderation. Grouse are half-gone from sight even before they're first seen, but the thunder of their flight echoes disturbingly in the ear. The hunter has no time to prepare for their sudden appearance, and scarcely a fraction of a second in which to mount the gun. At best, there is usually only one brief moment when a shot can be taken within honest gun range. The majority of the time (and this is statistical fact based on hunter surveys), ruffed grouse disappear before the gun can be raised and fired. The silence can be deafening.

The Ruffed Grouse in Flight

It is in flight that the ruffed grouse is most familiar to us. The standard going-away flushes are spectacular, but the rare sight of a coming-straight-at-you bird that has been flushed by another hunter is downright awe-inspiring. You might think that no bird would ever risk such scorching speeds amid the myriad tree trunks and branches of an upland covert. But then, when you observe how skillfully a grouse uses its broad fantail to steer around obstacles, it's easy to understand how this marvelous gamebird can so quickly dodge out of the hunter's line of sight.

Now you see it, now you don't. This magical quickness serves the grouse well when hawks or owls swoop to attack. In open woodlands, a grouse would be highly vulnerable to the birds of prey. In the typically thick tangles of a covert, however, the situation is altered. The grouse has a greater ability to veer and slip through the maze of its home turf on short, powerful wings. A skydiving raptor (with a wider wingspan) is apt to end up wearing a tree if it pursues too incautiously.

Grouse hunters, the human kind, are all too familiar with Ruff's talent for swerving behind a tree at the exact moment the trigger would have been pulled. This disappearing act, which seems only to be a purposeful evasion of the hunter's gun, is really an instinctual trait. For millennia, hawks and owls have been culling from the grouse population those birds that flew straight and slow. The survivors engendered the modern ruffed grouse—the one that so often outmaneuvers our own best predatory efforts.

We are inclined to compare the known swiftness of any bird or animal with established highway speed limits and to then make judgments of "slow" or "fast" based on current definitions of legal or illegal. The cheetah's ground charge, at seventy miles per hour or so, is considered by us to be awesomely fast. The falcon's dive, estimated to be in excess of a hundred miles per hour, is similarly thought to be an amazing feat. So, when we find that clocked measurements of grouse flights reveal rather modest speeds of thirty to fifty miles per hour, we feel somewhat disappointed.

These rates were determined with stopwatch and surveyor's tapes by investigators working on the famed New York study published in 1947. This prestigious and now highly collectible volume, *The Ruffed Grouse*, was compiled by Messrs. Bump, Darrow, Edminster, and Crissy. The information contained therein is just as valid today as it was when the field research was being done. There are many items of interest to the serious upland hunter, exactly 915 pages worth.

The fastest flight recorded in this study was 48.4 miles per hour over a distance just under 60 yards. But all the speeds were calculated *average* speeds for the entire distances flown. That is, no adjustment was made for the time required for grouse to get underway, to build up speed. If we look at the data from this perspective, the *real* final top speed of flight would be considerably greater than the average speed. It's not unreasonable to estimate sixty or even seventy miles per hour as being typical airspeed for a ruffed grouse once the initial acceleration is achieved. And that's downright respectable. But it's really the acceleration itself that makes the flush of a grouse such an incredible, even shocking, performance. Very few creatures on earth can match it, and not many hunters can reliably accelerate the swing of a gun's muzzle fast enough to beat it.

Of course, grouse do not always fly from Point A to Point B on a rolling crest of thunder that smashes the woodland stillness. The powerful flush is usually reserved for emergency escapes. Ruffed grouse are also capable of slow, silent flight, and they probably fly in this manner more often than most hunters realize. Certainly, if a grouse wants merely to flit up to the high branches of a poplar or cherry tree to feed on buds, an explosive flush would not be the best way to get there. Hunters seldom observe quiet flight; the grouse seems always in an extreme hurry to depart our company.

Grouse, the Terrestrial Bird

Despite its winged prowess and reputation as the gamebird most challenging to wingshooters, the ruffed grouse *(Bonasa umbellus)*, ironically spends most of its life on the ground. It belongs to the order Galliformes, which includes the pheasants, turkeys, quail, and domestic chickens. All these fowl are terrestrial birds, heavy of body and having stubby wings capable only of relatively short flights. None of them are migratory. Most rely on their ability to scratch and peck the ground for seeds and grains and whatever else they can find for food. But here a difference arises: the ruffed grouse is unique among gallinaceous fowl in its ability to thrive on a diet of the buds and leaves of certain trees and bushes. Other ground birds might starve on such fare, even if they were guided by instinct to seek it. For the ruffed grouse, there is almost always an ample supply of foods, even when bitter winter has covered the ground with snow. The winter buds of poplar, birch, wild cherry, and apple are notable examples. These are found most often in the crops of grouse shot on the days when winter has locked away fallen fruits and other edibles under a frozen blanket of white.

During most of the year, the grouse gets from one place to another by walking, even when it conveniently could have flown. Flight is potentially more dangerous, more apt to be detected by the eye of an overhead hawk, than is a discreet stroll under screening foliage. Only when a deep layer of soft, fluffy snow has fallen will grouse be inclined to journey under wing power. Even then, if the top layer of

The ruffed grouse is a "budder," unique in its ability to thrive on a winter diet of buds
from poplar, birch, wild cherry, and apple trees. In this photo, the bird's throat crop
has been removed to expose a mass of foraged buds.

loose snow is only a few inches deep, grouse will wade through it
rather than fly.

It is not uncommon to find shallow grooves in this type of snow
left by the snowplowing action of a meandering winter grouse. This is
not to say that unpressured grouse hardly ever fly. At any time of year,
Bonasa will spring into prolonged flight for a variety of reasons; yet
most days, grouse log but a few seconds of actual airborne time. They
fly from roost to the ground, and from ground to a perch among high-
hanging foods. That's just about the extent of it, except that this se-
quence is reversed shortly after sundown when grouse return to the
roost.

Ruffed grouse sometimes roost at night not in trees, but under the
insulating snow. And even during the midday hours, I have often
flushed grouse out from under the snow-bowed branches of "buckbrush," the same type of environment where a hunter would more
likely expect to spring a rabbit or two. Ruffed grouse are even more
apt to be found on terra firma when the cornucopia of autumn litters
the ground with a bounty of fruits and berries.

The New York State survey statistics for grouse flush origins show that only 10.8 percent of autumn grouse were flushed from trees. Even in winter, a mere 37.8 percent of grouse were found in trees, and no comment is made regarding the type of snow cover (if any) that prevailed when the flushes were recorded. Over the long haul of a year's time, 81.2 percent of the 3,057 grouse that flushed before on-coming researchers were *on the ground.*

What all this means to the hunter may not be as obvious to the neophyte as it is to the experienced upland gunner. When a grouse suddenly bursts into sight, it's usually already in flight, and we hardly ever stop to ponder the exact origin of the flush. Later, we may vaguely recall that the bird was "under something." But the tumultu-ous experience of trying to snap off a shot tends to erase most of the original details. If we miss with our shot(s) and subsequently strive for a reflush, the odds favor our finding the bird, now, in a tree. That's where grouse usually go when we give them, however inadvertently, a second chance.

The sum total of grouse hunting experience tells us, if we're not careful in our interpretations, that ruffed grouse are found "in flight" or "in a tree." But the most successful strategy for a grouse hunter is to search for grouse on the ground—or rather, to seek that type of habitat where grouse would have a reason to be on foot. For example, ruffed grouse seldom, if ever, will be flushed from the close-growing stems of goldenrod or meadow grasses. Pheasants maybe, but grouse, no. Similarly, rarely are grouse to be found on the floor of an open stand of hardwoods where they would be unnecessarily vulnerable to pre-dation. No, grouse are usually "under something."

They linger under bushes, overhanging evergreen boughs, grape-vine bowers, ferns, young poplars, hawthorn trees, and in any similar sun-sheltered place where the ground is relatively free of dense weed-growth. These secluded areas provide grouse with both shelter and easy access to a variety of foods. The existence of such open areas under the low, intermeshed branches of a covert is not always obvious at hunter's-eye level. A brush-choked gully, for example, may appear impenetrable, and yet the shallow stream that trickles along its length can be a virtual avenue for grouse traffic. The hunter's route through a grouse covert should approach as many of these hidden labyrinths as possible. With experience, a hunter can begin recognizing those types of vegetation which most likely harbor the out-of-sight hideaways where grouse lurk. An occasional grouse will be flushed now and then from wide open spaces, of course, and also from high in trees. But in the long run, a hunter will more often see grouse outlined against the sky if he first seeks his quarry on the ground.

Haunts and Habits

I once saw a grouse in a cage. I had heard about a fellow who raised all sorts of exotic fowl, pigeons and so on, and the word was out that he'd obtained and incubated several grouse eggs. Some of them had hatched and he had successfully raised one of the chicks to maturity. This was all highly illegal of course, but I was curious and wanted to see the bird.

I visited the fellow, did some talking, and he escorted me to the henhouse where the bird was kept. It looked like a grouse, but then again, it didn't. The bird's scalp was rubbed raw, apparently from countless attempts to spring up through the wire-mesh ceiling of its cage. There was less light in its eyes than I have seen in freshly killed wild grouse. It constantly paced the wire floor, cautious of my presence yet not looking at me. The feathered patterns were familiar and so was the quivering *cuk cuk!* alarm that the bird occasionally uttered. But if I had not already known that this sorry bird was a ruffed grouse, I could easily have been convinced that it was some sort of exotic Patagonian chicken that only looked like a grouse. I went away feeling vaguely disappointed.

The ruffed grouse I know is a winged fury, a quick blur against a cold sky, a demon of speed. Real grouse don't pace back and forth; they explode and are gone from sight before the dust can settle.

Several different attempts have been made by various state game agencies to artificially propagate the ruffed grouse for "stocking" purposes. These attempts have not been successful. Pheasant, quail, Hungarian partridge, and certain other gamebirds often are able to make the transition from domestic life to the wild world as soon as the lids of their transport crates are opened.

The ruffed grouse, however, seems to be so intricately geared to the mysterious inner workings of wild habitat that an early stint of domestic life dulls its ability to adapt properly. In the wild, the ruffed grouse is basically a loner. Grouse don't form flocks. In early autumn, several grouse might be flushed from under the same bush; but these are usually members of the immature brood of a single hen, which have not yet dispersed.

Wild grouse are also territorial creatures; the males each stake out their turf and drive all others away. Only during the brief rituals of springtime do adult grouse pair together for any specific reason other than fighting. Because of this maverick behavior, wild grouse lack the security provided by the collective awareness of large numbers. Yet the grouse compensates for its solitary ways with an instinctive wariness.

Sometimes the factors of weather or localized food supply will result in grouse temporarily congregating in the same corner of a covert. But when a hunter happens to discover a lode such as this, the birds will flush as individuals, each departing at a time and in a way that best serves its self-interests. It is this very trait of wary aloofness that makes the ruffed grouse the aristocrat of upland gamebirds. There is no worthier trophy. Certainly there are none harder to find, and none that present a more difficult target for the upland gunner.

In the hierarchy of grousedom, it is the adult male grouse who first establishes and then maintains the code of voluntary exile for all members of the species. In the spring of the year, victorious in his skirmishes with rival males and having evicted them from his tiny kingdom (about ten acres), the male grouse sets foot upon the drumming log and begins a strange and wonderful ritual. This is the drumming, the ever-faster beating of wings that creates brief rolls of thunder in the upland coverts. The sound of it has hollow, ghostly qualities that carry far and wide.

To the distant rival males, the sound of drumming is a warning to go peddle their genes somewhere else; but to the females of the covert, this wild rhythm is a beckoning. The hens come to watch the drummer and, if they aren't appropriately impressed, they go elsewhere in search of other drummers.

In the evolutionary scenario of *any* species, the traditional perspective says that the genetically superior male sets the standard. More recently, it has become fairly obvious that it is within the female's decision of whether or not to mate that the standards of supe-

The drummer on his log. *Photo by T. Martinson.*

riority are set. In the example of the ruffed grouse, perhaps the trait of antisocial behavior is fostered more by the female than by the male. Regardless, the end result is that ruffed grouse are generally spread at considerable distances from each other, with individual birds thriving or dying depending on their ability to maintain a hold on suitable habitat.

The male grouse also drums with a renewed vigor in the autumn, proclaiming to all creatures of the woodlands that the king of game-birds is once again reigning on his rotted-log throne. Young males hear the sound and take it as a warning to vacate that particular corner of the world. Dominant ruffed grouse will often challenge the apparent presence of *any* intruder. I've heard them drum in apparent response to the *whump!* of distant gunfire, to the sounds of car doors being slammed, branches being broken, farmers' tractors, and even to the sounds I purposely make by slapping my canvas-clad belly in an attempt to copy the sound of drumming.

I have read in many publications that a drumming grouse is super-wary; my personal experience tells me otherwise. Creeping up on the thunder bird is my way of picking up the gauntlet he's thrown in challenge. I figure I've won when I can just catch a glimpse of the bird before he flushes. Autumn drumming serves the purpose of maintaining a dispersion of all grouse, whether mature or juvenile, across the far reaches of available habitat. As winter nears and the supplies of food become less bountiful, grouse instinctively do what they must to achieve their own version of "wildlife management."

Cold wind, rain, snow: these elements of weather adversely affect the hunter more than they do the ruffed grouse. Many words have been logged in the annals of hunting literature regarding the right weather, the right direction of the wind, the right falling or rising of the barometer, and the right time of day for hunting our various game animals. In the face of this onslaught of well-intended information, we sometimes fail to recognize a very basic truth—that the game is always out there *somewhere* whether or not *we* are!

The ruffed grouse, in particular, is as huntable on the worst day of the year as on the best. Whereas many creatures of legal game status trek to distant hillsides or migrate south when chill winds bring unpleasant weather, the ruffed grouse merely hops to a branch on the leeward side of the current unpleasantness, or perhaps strolls a hundred yards or so along the ground to a more secure shelter.

Rain apparently bothers grouse less than falling snow, according to researcher Bump et al., and I suspect that this may have something to do with the reduced visibility which comes with heavy snowfall.

Grouse are more apt to be found in or near conifers when there's snow in the air and also when the temperature is unseasonably low. But a light rainfall seems to have little or no effect on grouse; their outer feathers shed most of the moisture. I have hunted several times during steady downpours, and on each occasion I have found Bonasa right where I would expect to flush him on bluebird days.

Time of day is another factor that influences where grouse will be found. But here again the differences in hours and yardages are nearly insignificant to the hunter. There are sufficient nuances in these differences to spawn a hundred "where-to-find-grouse" magazine articles. But the fundamental reality of grouse behavior is that the majority of these splendid gamebirds will be located in or near the places you found 'em last weekend. Hunt the familiar haunts first and reserve the formulas and enlightened techniques for later.

It's really food supply, rather than the clock or even the weather, that has the greatest influence on grouse habits. When it's winter and tree buds have become the main food source, grouse tend to feed in early morning and then again at sundown. This is not to say that grouse disappear from the face of the earth in between those two feeding times. After all, in most upland coverts there is no truly recognizable border between feeding and roosting areas. Such areas are intermingled very scenically (clumps of green conifers amidst the pale, probing limbs of birch and poplar), and rules-of-thumb for hunting winter grouse according to their feeding habits simply aren't practical. Especially in autumn, when the cornucopia of wild fruits is overflowing, grouse can be found virtually anywhere and at any time during daylight hours. You never know what you're going to find until that one extra step has been taken.

Grouse, it seems to me, are always on the move, except when they're asleep in a snowdrift or perched high on a tree branch. They wander much of the time, seeking one more bright berry, one more chance at survival of the species. Just because a hunter doesn't find grouse where he or she wants them to be doesn't mean that the birds won't be there a half hour later. The birds are usually not very far away anyway, if the covert is a good one. Even when the hunter is accompanied by a dog, a grouse that's just a few yards outside the dog's effective scenting range is one bird that "isn't there." But give that bird some time to meander a little farther along its chosen course, and the story may not be the same when hunter and dog head back to roadside. I often hunt the same covert twice when my first pass has failed to put up the birds that I know are there somewhere.

In spite of its elusiveness in flight, the ruffed grouse is a highly huntable bird. Let's put that another way: A good covert is a very huntable place. Several hours of hunting time can be productively spent in a covert that might not exceed the size of a nine-hole golf course. Most of us (myself included) tend to want to rush from one favored covert to the next when the birds seem to be OUT for the day. The fewer birds we've seen, the harder we press on the gas pedal and the less we try to avoid potholes in bumpy country roads along our way to where the birds might be IN. (Sound familiar?)

Yet, the very next time we get a chance to hunt, we head for that certain first place where grouse are known to lurk *some* of the time, believing or hoping that on this occasion our timing is proper and that the play of the fates will be on our side. Does it really matter, though, whether we hunt the same covert on two consecutive weekends . . . or twice within the same hour? I say *no!* Follow the same right path through a covert and, if there are grouse there anywhere, they will be encountered sooner or later. It doesn't matter how long it takes; time spent grouse hunting is never wasted.

The Ruffed Grouse Up Close

A grouse, dropped by gunfire and held in hand soon thereafter, represents a tension between the extremes of winning and losing. The warmth and softness of the bird are now in our possession, as is the limp heft of its feathered weight. But all we really wanted was to be able to control just one flickering moment during the thunderous, crashing seconds of a ruffed grouse's flight across a patch of sky. We used a gun to insert our soul into this picture, and this time it worked. A grouse fell into our ownership. Our prize is deserved, but it's sad that we had to kill to get that close to victory.

Most of us wouldn't be able to withstand the strain of a full-time job on the starting end of a meat-packing factory. But the typical ruffed grouse hunter is comfortable with the occasional act of killing game because, frankly, the element of pure luck is so very much involved. There is much more birdshot embedded in the trunks of trees still living than there are pellets that caused the ultimate passing of Bonasa. When we run our fingers over the still form of a freshly killed grouse, we experience several different emotions, not the least of which is sheer amazement at the turn of events. And there is a natural curiosity, too, because it's not all that often that a hunter gets a chance to hold a grouse for up-close scrutiny. It's like touching a dream, at least on those occasions which follow an extended shooting slump.

The average ruffed grouse is seventeen inches long, has a wing-span of about twenty-three inches, and weighs within an ounce of a pound and a half. Those are the vital statistics. Beyond this point, a uniqueness emerges. The ruffed grouse is totally different from all other gamebirds; moreover, no two individual grouse are exactly alike.

First, there is the matter of color. Grouse are categorized as being either red phase, grey phase, or a third "intermediate" phase. In reality, the possibilities for grouse coloration cover the entire spectrum from a light mottled silver all the way to a rich chocolate brown. (All grouse have barred white undersides.) As a rule of thumb, grouse from the northern reaches tend towards the grey phase, and they are found to be progressively more red towards the southern limits of their range. However, there are countless exceptions. All three color phases are hatched occasionally from the same clutch of eggs, anywhere north or south.

In western New York State where I do most of my grouse hunting, the majority of birds have orange-brown fantails and chestnut-colored bodies. I have shot only one silver phase grouse close to home, and the first fully red grouse I ever killed nearby was headed south—in a manner of speaking. This red bird flushed in New York State about thirty yards from the Pennsylvania border, and then veered towards Pittsburgh. I killed it in the air, right above the stone-marked border, and the bird plummeted into the other state. By my way of thinking, this event qualified as a "double."

Grey and intermediate phase grouse are apt to have black ruffs and tail bands, but on darker grouse these same features are more often a reddish brown.

Game biologists have conducted many surveys in attempts to explain these variations, but none has been able to derive a statistically based cause-and-effect relationship. Darker colored birds are more effectively camouflaged in the southerly forests, and grey birds obviously blend in better in the snowy regions. Still, the fact remains that any phase can (and does) appear at any location within the range of the ruffed grouse.

An even stranger variation can be seen in the patterns and markings of the grouse's plumage. These are not apparent when only one bird is being observed, but when two or more grouse are being examined the differences can be strikingly obvious. One grouse may display a wide tail band while another bird from the same covert has a very slender band. On some birds this dark fantail band is bordered by a wide secondary band of mottled white, and on others, it is not.

Other textured patterns on the fantail can vary greatly from bird to

bird. I have seen several grouse that had such a profusion of creamy
white feathers around their shoulders that they looked more like the
results of an Arctic ptarmigan outcrossing than pure ruffed grouse.
Sizes of certain markings also vary; often the typical light-on-dark is
reversed to dark-on-light.

Despite these seemingly infinite variations of color and pattern,
there's no mistaking the identity of the ruffed grouse. The square tail
that can be spread 180 degrees into a rounded fan is the feature most
easily recognized in flight. But the broad, square feathers with the
dark metallic sheen—the ruff that the "ruffed" grouse sports atop each
shoulder just above the wings—are the source of its name. Somewhat
more apparent on the male of the species, the ruff becomes flared
during courtship and whenever a display is needed for the sake of
territorial defense.

In preparation for winter, a longer growth of insulating feathers
appears on the grouse's upper legs and a series of tiny appendages
develops along the edges of the bird's toes. These appendages, assem-
bled like the teeth on a comb, have long been thought by biologists to
serve as "snowshoes." But more likely, they help the grouse to grasp
cold winter tree limbs, sometimes ice-covered, as it forages for nutritious buds.

Like most gallinaceous fowl, the ruffed grouse has a crop under
its throat for the temporary storage of food. It's not visible even when
crammed full, but the hunter's probing fingers can easily detect the

The feathered ruff of the "ruffed" grouse is usually black, sometimes brown.

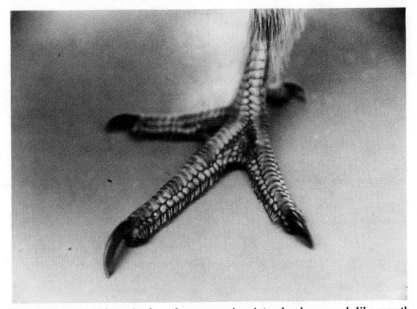

For a more secure grip on icy branches, grouse in winter develop a comb-like growth along the edges of each toe.

crop under the skin if the bird has recently been feeding. As I explain later in this book, identification of the contents of a grouse's crop provides useful clues to the whereabouts of other grouse.

Most grouse hunters are curious about the age and sex of a bird they have killed because such information has relevance to the overall vitality and abundance of that season's bird population. For example, if the majority of birds killed are juveniles, then we may infer that the spring hatch has been a good one. Also, if a fellow takes two or three females out of a small favorite covert (the luck of the draw somehow keeping the males out of his shot pattern), he will, as a responsible hunter, take his gun elsewhere to avoid destroying the potential for next year's hunting.

Determining whether a fallen grouse is a juvenile or an adult bird is not easy; they're all in the same size group by October. "Little" or "big" carries no meaning here; full skeletal growth and plumage development are achieved in the first six months of life. The tips of a juvenile's primary wing feathers are sharply tapered. And if one of these feathers is plucked, flakes of residual sheathing will be seen still attached to the quill. Older grouse have blunted wingtips and the quills won't show any sheathing.

The two dots on this bird's rump feathers indicate the male sex. This is confirmed by the tail band, which in this photo is unbroken across the two center tail feathers.

Determining the sex of a grouse is much easier. There are several different ways to do it. All of the following methods are reliable, but only the last one is foolproof.

The classic way to determine the sex of a ruffed grouse is to look at the *tail band*, that broad, dark stripe that parallels the edge of the fan. If the two center feathers don't show the band markings, the grouse is probably a female. But be aware that many males display a blurred version of the band on these two feathers. Only if the band is completely broken can the bird be considered a female.

The bold presence of ruff feathers on the grouse's shoulders is not adequate indication of its gender. Males generally have more prominent ruffs, but it's difficult to establish a ruffed grouse's sex here. Look elsewhere.

The *rump dot* method works with much greater certainty. The feathers on a grouse's rump, just above the stiff covert feathers that form a mini-fan atop the fantail, have one or more white dots on them. One dot means that the bird is a female. If there are two (or sometimes even three) dots on a single feather, the bird is almost certainly a male.

The *eye patch* directly above a grouse's eyelid is another fairly reliable indicator of the bird's sex. To view this small patch of bare skin, gently push the feathers upward, away from the eye. If the eye patch is pale red or orange, the bird is a male. Hen grouse show no coloration here.

Another method which hunters seldom (if ever) use, but which biologists have established as being surefire at least 95 percent of the time, is the *tail feather length* measurement. The two middle tail feathers, the same ones that make or break the band, are longer than 5⅞ inches if the bird is a male. If these feathers are shorter than 5½ inches, the bird is a female.

None of the preceding methods is totally reliable, since the visible differences between male and female in ruffed grouse are very subtle. (The male grouse's drumming suffices as proper and acceptable identification during the breeding season.) The only infallible method for determining sex is to check the internal reproductive organs. This isn't as difficult or as technical as it might seem; the bird has to be gutted anyway.

In both sexes, these organs are located on either side of the spine, at the front ends of the kidneys. The ovaries in a hen grouse are usually a little over a quarter-inch long, and they resemble a tight cluster of miniature white grapes. Most often, the ovary is fully developed only on the hen's left side. The male testes, however, will be seen on both sides of the spine, partially hidden in a light-colored tissue. The testes are smooth and greyish in appearance. If the male bird is a juvenile, the testes will be darker and smaller.

The eye patch beneath the feathers is pale red or orange on male grouse.

Grouse eggs are laid on the ground, usually at the base of a tree or stump.

Grouse Renewal: Nesting and Brooding

Once the tryst in the shadow of the drumming log is over, the hen grouse goes her own way, sometimes travelling up to half a mile or so before selecting a place to nest the forthcoming eggs. She will raise next year's grouse without help from the male.

The nesting site is usually at the base of a tree or stump in the sort of habitat often not recognizable as "grouse cover." The nest itself is merely a rounded depression made to fit the hen's contours, in plain sight of all the woodland world and yet invisible to eyes that cannot distinguish between leaf litter and dappled feathers. The eggs, usually one or two short of an even dozen, are laid one at a time over a two-week period. They're the color of cream.

The only humans, I'm convinced, that ever discover grouse nests are wildlife researchers and spring turkey hunters. No one else seems to go into the woods at this delicate time of the year. If by chance the nest is approached too closely, too directly, the hen will flee, sometimes feigning injury, but more often in typical grouse fashion: fast. One tends to "watch the birdie" and not think of a nest nearby.

As with all birds, the hen doesn't begin incubating until all the eggs are laid. This insures that they'll all hatch on the same day, which is usually in late May or early June. Newly hatched grouse are precocious little creatures. As soon as they're dry, the mother hen leads her chicks off in search of more suitable habitat. The chicks begin eating small insects along the way, and within ten days are even able to fly. After about a month, the chicks switch from their diet of insects to the tender green shoots and berries that become abundant in early summer.

Traditionally, grouse hunters have believed that wet, cold weather during nesting and brooding is an omen of poor autumn hunting. But harsh weather actually has minimal influence on brood survival. In fact, as Dr. Gordon Gullion points out in his book, *Grouse of the North Shore*, studies have shown no connection at all between spring weather and the subsequent population of autumn grouse. Instead, there seems to be a correlation with the weather and habitat of the preceding winter. Winter is the time of year when everything either works right or not at all.

Dispersal

Within 15 to 16 weeks after hatching, the young grouse are completely grown and fully feathered. And they're ready to find a place in the world for their very own. The fall dispersal of ruffed grouse is Nature's effective way of insuring that every suitable covert annually has a renewed opportunity to host the ruffed grouse. The flock begins

A one-week-old grouse chick.

to break up in mid-September, with the young birds striking off in separate directions. Usually the males leave first; but the females travel farther, often several miles, thus helping to additionally scatter the species' genes far from the family pool.

Although the phenomenon of "crazy flight" is popularly associated with the autumn dispersal, grouse generally get to their ultimate destinations on foot. They walk for several days, alone and vulnerable. Apparently they fly recklessly when frightened, which explains the myriad accounts of grouse exploding through kitchen windows or entangling themselves in farmers' fences. The young birds have not yet learned many of the harsh realities of independence. Many grouse die along the route. Some, because the choice of direction was a poor one, never arrive in suitable habitat. In early autumn, the hunter will occasionally flush grouse from any and all varieties of habitat. Grouse are often located where they shouldn't be, and a neophyte hunter can get the wrong idea about the ideal grouse habitat. But the autumn dispersal is finished in late October; by the end of November, all surviving birds will have found refuge in proper habitat.

3

What Is a Covert?

What is a covert? Well, a covert is where grouse are. And where there are ruffed grouse, there will also be found all of the elements necessary to their survival. But these answers beg the question. A covert represents more than a mere balance of habitat; it is a *haunted* place where sometimes silent mornings echo with the ghostly drumming sound of wings blurred in motion.

A covert is a possession of the mind, of memories, a special place where the hunter walks, knowing that at any instant a ruffed grouse can shatter tranquility and thereby stake claim to a share of that ownership. You recognize the existence of a covert by the technical aspects of habitat, and confirm it as such by flushing grouse there. But given a locale, a known domain of grouse, no two grouse hunters will perceive the borders of said covert by identical landmarks; nor will they see the inner workings of the covert by the same patterns of expectant densities.

One hunter may visualize a covert as being defined along one edge by a meandering creek, while his partner instead sees the creek as the focal point of the covert. One fellow expects that a grouse will flush over by the barberries; the other strides along through this prickly growth confident of producing a flush past where the barberries end and stretches of grapevines begin. Each has memories of past and personal encounters with grouse. Whether this covert is a new discovery or a territory made familiar by a decade's wanderings, it will be known to each hunter separately in direct measure to his past encounters with ruffed grouse.

Biologists call coverts "perennial activity centers" and define them in accordance with known food and shelter preferences of grouse. My dictionary says that a covert is "a hiding place; a thicket affording cover for game." It makes no mention whatsoever of *Bonasa umbellus.* The individual grouse hunter, drawing from personal experience more than from any other source, creates a definition that has real meaning only to him. It is not sufficient to merely indicate a wooded locale with a casual wave of the arm and say, "That is a grouse covert." Perhaps in the next few pages we can come up with a description that has meaning for all of us.

Sizes of Coverts

There is one particular overgrown corner of a pasture near where I live that invariably produces at least one flushing grouse whenever I hunt it. The blackberry tangles there are as treacherous in places as concertina, but the rutted remnants of two old logging roads which intersect near the center provide easy access—except where a few ancient hemlocks have toppled. Young poplars and several wild cherry trees grow in this grouse nook, and there are a number of conifers (white pines, I think) clumped together here and there with boughs that hang nearly to the ground.

This corner is truly a haven for ruffed grouse during all the seasons of the year. Hen grouse nest in the adjacent hardwoods, just on the other side of a barbed-wire fence. (The posts have rotted so the fence tilts, awaiting my voluntary annual repairs with propped sticks.) Cattle seldom venture into this domain unless bent on escape. Winter cover in the form of a forbidding hemlock swamp is provided for grouse on two other sides of the corner, and open pasture spans the remaining edge. Year after year, I kill three or four grouse in this corner and still leave as many or more birds there to breed in the spring.

How big is this grouse hunter's utopia? About three acres, that's all. The outer regions occasionally produce a grouse or two, but only sporadically and at the expense of much legwork. If I were to be placed in a situation where I absolutely had to find a grouse, this is where I'd go. From the viewpoint of a grouse hunter, I see this magic little pasture corner as being a complete covert. But as an interested student of grouse habitat, I know that the surrounding woodlands are essential parts of its productivity. (Point of interest: A square acre is approximately seventy yards per side.)

The corner covert exists in my mind as a definable unit almost as surely as if it were bordered by velvet rope hung on brass standards. I know when I'm in it, and my hunter's mind knows when I take the first step out of the covert. (To protect these presumptions, I consider any bird that flushes from where it shouldn't to be a "stray.") Understand that this little covert is close to home, and that I go there often for dog training exercises and for wildlife photography, in addition to hunting. I have learned through experience where grouse will usually flush and in which direction they will go. But consider this: I am seldom afforded what could fairly be described as a decent shot! Even though the covert is scarcely big enough to hold two football gridirons, there is plenty of room available for grouse in flight to maneuver into the safety of the adjoining hemlocks or hardwoods. Just as surely as I know when I'm in the pasture covert, so do the grouse; they can see me coming.

A covert such as this one is worth an hour's walk through unproductive cover to reach. And it's worth an hour's hard hunting once you get there. This might seem strange—that a very small covert could justify such a lengthy investment in your time—but it's true. Stalking slowly and cautiously is what's needed to properly hunt small, strategically placed coverts. Pass through too quickly, too boldly, and grouse will remain hunkered down out of sight until you're gone. The birds are there; you just never know *exactly* where.

On the other hand, down the hill from this covert, on the far side of the hardwood lot, there is a larger, forty-acre square of thornapples, poplars, and feral apple trees bordered along one edge by thick hemlocks. I often find grouse here in this technically balanced habitat; but despite the considerably greater size of the area, the birds are almost always to be found in the same small places. (As with the pasture corner, it's close by and I go there often.) The grey dogwood bushes around the old dead elm are always worth checking, and so is the shaded fenceline. Ironically, I have only once flushed a grouse out from under the low-hanging branches of the cluster of apple trees;

The actual size and boundaries of a ruffed grouse covert are known only in the minds of the hunters and dogs who go there.

here I place autumn apples in my gamebag—not grouse. The brushy fringes along the hemlocks and a certain stretch of high ground alongside a shaded little bog are the only other regions of this forty-acre patch that appear to be inhabited by grouse. Nevertheless, I consider the whole patch to be a covert. I can't in good faith ignore those remaining acres of good habitat, even though grouse never seem to go there. I do, they don't. If the word "covert" is taken literally as meaning a place to hide, then perhaps I should consider only those few acres where grouse are found as the true area of the covert. Maybe so; it's a question worthy of debate by the fireside, but I already know that there would be no clear winners.

There's another forty-acre covert that I often hunt, almost a duplicate but several miles distant, in which grouse can be flushed from almost anywhere. From the moment I step off the roadside, I am on full alert and *hunting*. There is an elemental difference between these two essentially identical coverts, but it's one that I have not yet identified. Perhaps it is no coincidence that this second forty-acre plot is also the sweetest I've ever found for early season woodcock.

Most of the coverts that I visit at least once each season are smaller than forty acres, scarcely the size of the parking lot of a sub-urban shopping mall. Each of these ruffed grouse coverts is sur-rounded by woodlands that no doubt are part of the covert's ecosys-tem, but you'll seldom find grouse more than the distance of a flush away from the central covert areas.

I also have a few places on my ever-growing list of coverts (yes, I do keep a list) that encompass well over a hundred acres. That is to say, I walk routes which encircle at least that much area, and I'm apt to flush grouse from almost any point along the way. Even as I write this, though, I realize that I had mentally subdivided these larger grouse coverts into much smaller ones, each having their own name and identity.

We could argue that the size of a grouse covert should be meas-ured not in acreage, but in the *length of the route* required to touch bases with all the known hotspots. Yes, this concept could spark debates that might very well have winners! The value of edge cover to wildlife is known by every experienced hunter. Fencerows, the brushy edges of mature forests, overgrown creek banks, pasture corners, and any other natural interruptions of uniform habitat create a needed diversity of food and shelter for grouse and other creatures. Even the vast poplar and coniferous woodlands of southern Canada and the northern Great Lakes regions are transected by logging roads and other breaks. It is along these departures from monotonous cover that ruffed grouse—and grouse hunters—are most apt to be found.

The path we follow through a familiar covert is, like life itself, a succession of maybes, with some stretches carrying more expectant hopes than others. Perhaps this is why a newly discovered covert is so enjoyable to hunt; we have not yet had a chance to locate those myste-rious voids in the action, those tempting-looking little pieces of cover that perpetually fail to contain grouse.

Why this concern of mine over the true dimensions of grouse coverts? I am motivated to expound on this particular subject because of the fact that so much of the material already written and published about grouse hunting does not tell you, for example, that being a single yard too far away from a certain sumac bush is also three feet short of flushing a grouse. Hunting without a dog, I could easily follow certain routes through my favorite coverts and be fairly certain that nary a grouse would show itself. I could avoid certain thickets, pass quickly through known hotspots without a purposeful hesitation in my stride, and perhaps stay clear of certain tantalizing clumped pines. That's the way to *not* find grouse in their coverts. And yet, all the while, I would be surrounded by many of the necessary elements of grouse habitat: poplars, pines, fruit trees, and berry and herb bushes.

I maintain that the size of a grouse covert can only be measured by the length of the loose thread that pulls the tapestry of it all together. This thread is the path that an experienced grouse hunter will follow, after he has had a chance to hunt and study a new covert. Almost every haunt of ruffed grouse contains a narrow corridor along which grouse are most vulnerable to the approaching hunter. When you discover this corridor, this right path, you will have gained possession of a covert.

Some Technical Aspects of Grouse Habitat

I have a little problem here. The elements of grouse habitat have, on the one hand, been so thoroughly researched by wildlife biologists and other scientists that it seems there are precious few secrets left. Reams of data have revealed that ruffed grouse have some very specific food and shelter preferences, and that their behavior under certain circumstances is highly predictable. On the other hand, there are the many exceptions, those minor percentages and accumulated deviations which combine to make the *hunting* of grouse a sport with uncertain results. And that is as it should be. Such unpredictability makes translating the technical aspects of habitat into something both meaningful and useful to the lay hunter a less than easy task.

Even if you play the odds right and are able to use the data to find just the right combinations of food and cover, those same odds are often leaned against you. For example, that prodigious volume of grouse research, *The Ruffed Grouse*, by Bump, Darrow, Edminster, and Crissey, contains within its depths the fact that the most popular food of autumn grouse in my home state (New York) is thornapples. But "most popular" was only 11.8 percent of total foods eaten, a far cry from an overwhelming majority. The next nine most-often-consumed foods were (in descending order of popularity) beechnuts, birch buds, apples, cherries, hop-hornbeam, viburnum berries, strawberry leaves, sumac, and dogwood berries. The percentages for all of these (including thornapples), add up to only 62.8 percent; the mysterious remaining "Other" is probably where all the grouse were congregated the last time I was afield in the statistically proper cover and not able to find a single grouse. If you hadn't just read this and you were new to New York State and if you believed me that thornapples are the favorite food of grouse, you would probably pass up nearly 90 percent of other cover where the hunting might be just as good.

The thornapple (also known as hawthorn) is armed with sharp spikes. Over 550 species and varieties have been identified within the range of the ruffed grouse.

Of course, on the dank, sweet earth under a thornapple patch, nearly 100 percent of autumn grouse there are feeding on thornapples. But in a dogwood thicket, their crops are plump with dogwood berries. And in an abandoned apple orchard, you'd reasonably expect grouse to be feeding on apples. And so on. You find grouse where they happen to be. It has even been argued that the various percentages of wild foods found in grouse crops are not really measures of grouse *preferences* as much as they are an indication of overall *availability* of these seasonal foods. One year, a late spring frost killed all the thornapple blossoms in some of my favorite coverts. That October, *none* of the grouse there were able to partake of this particular delicacy.

Probably the most nutritious food available to the ruffed grouse is supplied by poplar trees, particularly the species known as quaking aspen or "popple." The smooth white of its bark and the shimmering yellow of its autumn leaves are giveaway clues to the existence of many hidden grouse coverts. Grouse feed on the buds of mature poplars from late fall to late winter, and on the catkins that flower from

Grey dogwood berries are white in autumn.

these buds in springtime. The new green leaves that begin to swell as daylight increases are yet another source of wholesome food. Thickets of young poplar whips and saplings also provide grouse with a protective screen from the swooping attacks of hawks.

Poplar trees are as common as weeds throughout most of the range of the ruffed grouse, and yet, there is a sour note involved in this seeming harmony of bird and tree. Grouse populations are known to experience their sharpest up-and-down swings where poplar buds are the primary winter food. One possible reason for this is the occasional but wholesale presence of certain chemicals in the gummy resin which coats the scales on winter poplar buds. Why this occurs is not yet known; but Nature is perpetually impatient with takers who don't give in return, and grouse contribute nothing to poplar survival. (Grouse do contribute to the dissemination of wild cherry, thornapple, and dogwood, transporting their hard, heavy seeds over far greater distances than would otherwise occur. Thus, new coverts sometimes sprout from old droppings.)

In a balanced habitat, the poplar tree is nevertheless a panacea to the problem of grouse survival. Even though the chemical changes in the bud resins cause a grouse population to plummet, their numbers drop only to what would be considered "normal" anyplace else. In other words, a low population in poplar habitat equates to an average or even good population in other types of grouse cover. According to some scientifically based projections, grouse can be as much as five to ten times as abundant in a poplar habitat during peak years. Obviously, the poplar has much to offer the ruffed grouse.

The spring catkins and early summer leaves are never affected by the chemicals that sometimes taint bud resins in winter. The awesome regenerative properties of poplars supply an ever-renewing quality to established coverts, if properly managed by cutting or by controlled fire. Poplars usually grow as clones, sharing genes and a common ancestory via an underground root system that can encompass several acres. There are male and female poplars (they don't really *do it*, of course), but all the trees in a particular group of clones will be of the same sex. This is important from a game and habitat management point of view, because it is the male poplar that produces the nutritious buds rich in fats, proteins, and minerals.

The poplar tree (aspen) is both a source of food for grouse, and a sign to the hunter of good habitat. Bright yellow autumn leaves and white trunk can be seen for miles.

Winter buds on a poplar tree.

When a mature poplar tree is felled, hundreds of new stems begin shooting upward from the root system. These young growths provide a dense and protective cover for little grouse chicks in their quest for insects and tender green shoots. As the male clones grow taller and the outer branches gain a mature rigidity suitable for perching, a renewed bounty of buds becomes available to hungry grouse.

That's how grouse habitat can be managed: by literally killing the goose that laid the golden egg, but without our having to pay the consequences of that little fable. Grouse habitat is always associated with regenerative growth. Abandoned farmlands, covered strip mines, the sites of logging operations, and even the charred scars of forest fires will quickly enter the early stages of forest succession. Dozens of varieties of herbs, briars, and bushes miraculously gain a foothold on the bare turf; but they are soon partially shaded by fast-growing trees such as evergreens, hawthorns, hop-hornbeam, and the ubiquitous poplar. Not until a half century later will the slower growing hardwoods finally block the sunlight with their towering crowns, bringing to an end the life of a balanced grouse covert.

Poplars are present in nearly all the coverts in my own corner of grouse range, but never in quantities that would make them the major source of food. Occasionally I find poplar buds in a winter-killed grouse, but I usually find instead the dark slender buds of wild cherry or the squat, light brown buds of apple and hawthorn. I still consider poplars to be a very important element in the habitat of these coverts. If nothing else, they provide "my" grouse with the kind of densely packed vertical cover through which the birds can more safely stroll in search of other foods.

Even though poplar trees are often not a major component of habitat in the major share of the range they share with the ruffed grouse, these trees still offer the hunter a special clue to the where-abouts of grouse. Where you find poplars, you will also find the type of early stage, forest growth frequented by grouse. Poplars are easy to see from a distance—a whole lot easier than grouse! The bright solid yellow of poplar leaves in autumn and the slender white trunks grow-ing in thick clusters are easy to spot from a roadside vista or a distant ridge.

Water supply and topography are two other elements of grouse habitat; neither of these holds much importance for the hunter. We tend to visualize the ideal grouse covert as having a picturesque little creek burbling down through it. Wildlife artists and many outdoor writers are inclined to run creeks through coverts because, well, peo-ple like creeks and figure that grouse do too. Yes, it's true that grouse need water, but they seldom need to *drink* it. Most of the herbs, leaves, and fruits that grouse eat already contain more than fifty per-cent water. When that's not enough, such as in winter when the birds are on comparatively dry rations, there's always snow or rain for a bit of supplementary moisture. In a normal summer, there's also dew available.

During a very dry year, grouse may be found in the lush vegeta-tion along a creek bank, or under the fern fronds of a mucky swale. It's usually not the water that draws grouse to these places, but the types of plants that are associated with moist areas. Except for the influence which a creek (or a swamp, alder run, or any other source of wetness) might have on the availability of food resources, there's no reason to paint some water into your personal picture of a covert. Maybe your dog enjoys wallowing in muddy pools on a hot day; grouse don't.

Topography has been similarly overrated by some outdoor writers and many dedicated hunters, both groups hell-bent on wringing the last bit of goodness out of the dry data of research. The facts are that (1) a *few* more grouse than usual have been found to flush from north-facing slopes during the midday hours, and (2) in winter, a significant number of grouse are apt to be found on east-facing slopes and in valley bottoms. Mind you, these places are not where *all* the grouse go, but just more than the average.

No one, including the researchers, seems to have an explanation for why some grouse spend noon on a northern slope. Maybe the birds prefer to rest in some sheltered spot at this time of day, and perhaps it is no coincidence that evergreens tend to grow on north-facing slopes. If that's the case, then my interpretation is that the hunter at midday should concentrate on hunting conifers, regardless of which slope they happen to be growing on. But thanks for the invitation; I eat lunch then anyway.

There's not much mystery surrounding the ruffed grouse's decided preference for east slopes in winter. They go there to get out of the wind. So do you. East-facing slopes are on the leeward side of the prevailing wind, which any creature with at least half its normal instincts intact will try to avoid when the weather turns cold. Of course, when an occasional blizzard or cold weather front comes in from a different direction, more grouse will be found on the leeward side of whatever direction is needed to stay warm. That is, they will relocate if the size of their covert is large enough to contain more than one slope. If it isn't, the grouse will just move a little deeper into heavy cover.

There has also been much research done on the importance of drumming log sites to the viability of a covert. If the male grouse doesn't have a suitable log—of certain dimensions, located in just the right combination of both protective and projective surroundings—he cannot successfully advertise his desirability to receptive hens in early springtime. No log equals no chicks. Wildlife managers have even made efforts to construct concrete "logs," so important is this element of grouse habitat.

However, I don't recommend making the search for drumming logs an important part of your quest for new coverts. If you can find grouse in a covert, rest assured there's at least one good log there somewhere. Maybe several. I believe that the grouse hunter is naturally interested in locating the drumming sites in his coverts, but such knowledge is not essential to an understanding of where ruffed grouse can be found on Opening Day.

In the final analysis, the scientific study of grouse habitat is more relevant to developing habitat improvement programs than it is to helping the individual hunter to flush a bird or two. Just about the time you figure that all the statistical puzzles have finally fitted together, something offbeat will happen to shake your faith in the scien-

Ruffed grouse behavior and habitat have been well-researched, but the birds themselves are individually unpredictable. A raised crest indicates that this grouse will probably flush at any instant—but the hunter won't know in which direction until the event occurs. *Photo by T. Martinson.*

tific method. A grouse will unexpectedly flush from the closely cropped grass of an open pasture where it was probably feasting on meadow mushrooms. Or, you'll kick a whole living *herd* of grouse out of the ditch beside your parked vehicle. I've seen few enough grouse in open hardwoods to know that these places aren't worth hunting seriously, but I've killed a number of birds in just this kind of setting while on my way elsewhere.

The autumn dispersal of young flocks also contributes to the birds being placed where they don't really belong ecologically. Dispersal is a randomized event, and some grouse simply choose the wrong direction when their otherwise reliable instincts say it's time to go. A hunter never knows with certainty whether or where a grouse can be found until it is actually seen—and neither do the wildlife researchers. Sure, you can greatly improve your odds at finding grouse by heeding the advice implied in the charts and tables of habitat research. Don't, however, make the mistake of excluding from your pathway those elements of habitat which fall low on the charts. Be ready for the unexpected because that's what grouse hunting is all about. Walk those extra exploratory miles, seek new and different types of cover, and learn from your experiences. Every covert is unique, every hunter is an individual; and despite the massive amount of research that has been done, every grouse flush is still a surprise.

4

Getting the Most Out of a Covert

Finding the Loose Thread

One of grouse hunting's better moments begins when we take that first step into a new covert. At that particular point in time, we have no way of knowing with certainty whether this will be the first of many future visits, or a one-time proposition which will fizzle out because the right combinations of habitat aren't present. Not knowing which side of the coin will be uncovered, we nevertheless proceed, one expectant step at a time, into unknown territory. Slowly we move, observing with greater detail here than on the home ground of familiar coverts, discovering mere branches rather than valleys. Our senses are never more alert than when stalking a new covert.

When first exploring a new covert, an experienced grouse hunter will pay more attention to the orientation of the habitat than to his hunting technique. The grip on the gun will be a little less tense, and the steps forward will not be as purposeful. The whole idea behind this initial endeavor is to learn the lay of the land, to determine whether there is sufficient balance of seasonal habitat to maintain a grouse population, and then finally, to seek that loose thread, the magic deadly corridor. That's where the grouse will be found.

Sure, a fellow can plunge into a new covert and do nothing but *hunt*, heading for likely grouse haunts and caring little or nothing about magic corridors and all that stuff. Sometimes this headlong approach works just as well as the more careful alternative. Why take a chance on wasting time when you can be getting results, right? Well, maybe not. As with getting icecubes out of a tray or a scared bird dog into a car crate, using the headlong approach to impose your will upon a covert tends to backfire. Too many steps get taken while, ironically, too few grouse are usually moved.

A good grouse covert is like a fine wine (perhaps cider would be more appropriate) in that it improves in proportion to your appreciation of its subtleties. Such appreciation comes only with experience.

Look first for food, then for shelter. Depending on the time of day and the turn of the season, grouse will be found close by one or the other. Remember, there must be a *balance* of habitat. I know of one potential covert that could support a thousand or more grouse in October, but would be starvation headquarters for more than a half dozen grouse come December. Hawthorns grow here in thick profusion, covering several hundred acres of long-deserted pasture, and there are many places where barberry bushes grow so close together that even a dog must circle them. An ancient orchard stands along a stretch of the meandering stream that drains this picturesque slope. Literally tons of fruit and berries rot on the ground each year; songbirds and whitetail deer gorge here and still leave a bounty that persists only until snowfall locks it away.

This seemingly rich covert has, unfortunately, a very weak link in the chain of seasonal habitat. There is virtually no winter cover here, no poplars to supply nutritious buds for hungry grouse in January and February, and no clusters of young bushy evergreens for protection against hawks and cold winds. But this is not the end of the bad news for this unbalanced covert. It is an island of sorts, surrounded on three sides by large bare pastures and tilled fields, and on the fourth by an eighteen-hole golf course. Any grouse that manages to arrive here as a result of the early autumn dispersal of broods is destined first for feast, and soon afterwards for famine.

I hunted this so-called covert several times before I finally realized why there were so few grouse in such a lovely place. Woodcock were always there, however, feeding probably on the choice fruit-sweetened worms; the pleasant diversion these small brown birds offered was sufficient to temporarily alter my course towards finding better grouse cover.

Putting woodcock aside (and that's not easy for me to say), prospecting for grouse habitat can be as enjoyable as gunning the bird. The veteran grouse hunter has to be more knowledgeable about the technical features of game habitat than the average hunter. Rabbits can be found almost anywhere in brushy cover, and so can deer and other gamebirds such as pheasant and quail. Squirrels and wild turkeys are somewhat more specific in their requirements, but finding nut trees is no big deal for the hunter who has taken the time to learn what beech, oak, or hickory trees look like.

The ruffed grouse hunter needs to be much more informed about *combinations* of habitat before he can reliably locate the kind of cover where grouse reign. But there is an apparent paradox here. Ruffed grouse are known to eat literally hundreds of different types of wild foods; they dine regularly (in season) on such diverse foods as tree buds, beechnuts, berries, clover, and even mushrooms. You would expect that with such an easy-to-please palate, grouse could survive almost anywhere. But they can't—at least not for very long. The seasonal sprouting and ultimate withering of food varieties are as inexorable as the annual wobble of the earth on its axis. We tend to think that harvest time is limited only to autumn, but in actuality there is a perpetual shifting forward to new and different varieties of wild food harvests.

The sharp cold of winter triggers a burgeoning of highly nutritious tree buds, of which poplar and wild cherry are notable examples. Grouse can survive and even thrive during the meanest of winters when buds are easily available to them. As time slides a spring thaw across a grouse covert, new growths appear, each in its own special day or week and in a slightly different part of the covert. Fern sporeheads appear along with other delectable green shoots and leaves. Various herbs, some early and some delayed depending upon their genetic inner windings, sprout in time to keep the early summer cornucopia flowing. Wild strawberries ripen under the sun in far greater abundance than many people realize.

The autumn season opens the door to a virtual torrent of ripe fruits and berries, and it is then that we find grouse gorging themselves under the dogwood and viburnum bushes, the hawthorn and crabapple trees, the wood's edge beeches, and the grapevine bowers. Upon discovering such autumn feeding activity, we exclaim, "Aha! A new covert!" We tend to think only in terms of the present condition of the habitat and ignore its seasonal shifts.

A good grouse covert will contain a seasonably balanced supply of wild foods close to protective shelter. This scene of a covert includes poplars and thornapples banked up against evergreens.

The grouse's diet is definitely a moveable feast with an ever-changing menu. But the ruffed grouse is a nonmigratory bird, limited by short, stubby wings that are useful for only brief, explosive flights. And time spent traveling in search of available foods makes a grouse vulnerable to predation. Foraging must be done quickly and discreetly, not far from evening's roosting place. Consequently, a "good" grouse covert must contain, within its narrow boundaries, a seasonally balanced supply of wild foods in proximity to protective shelter. The greatest potential a covert has for grouse survival is measured there by the weakest link in the chain of food production. Most other wild game species are far more mobile in their quests for food.

A grouse hunter prospecting a new covert knows he has struck gold when the basic elements of four-season habitat are present. Even if no grouse are flushed during those initial explorations, a fellow can forge ahead the next time with a happy confidence that he will indeed find grouse when he discovers *the right way to hunt the covert*.

To accomplish this, I believe that the covert should be hunted thoroughly, as though there were a bird under every bush. Approach each nook and cranny with the certainty that a grouse is about to flush. Having that optimistic attitude, you will begin asking yourself very important questions, such as, "If I move in from this direction, will I be able to see the grouse when it flushes?" And, "Which way will it probably go?"

Grouse hunting is much like a lifesize game of chess, in which the strategies of position often aren't revealed until several moves later. The ruffed grouse is usually reluctant to flush until all his other options are cut off. Basically a ground dweller, a grouse prefers either to rely on his natural camouflage as a first line of defense or to simply walk away from possible danger.

It's my opinion that a grouse already knows from which directions safety beckons. I just can't imagine that avenues of escape aren't preplanned when so much is at stake. The grouse, lurking in concealment, no doubt is prepared with his own package of instinctive strategies when your impending approach is first detected. How you play *your* next move will be crucial. Pass innocently past the wrong side of a tree, and the sudden sound of wings from the other side will signal that Old Ruff has cleaned the board with a solid checkmate!

By bringing an optimistic attitude into a new covert and expecting to find grouse there, you will gradually develop a pattern of subtle awarenesses. Imagination is a useful learning tool, and so is past experience when correctly applied in new situations. If you constantly question yourself as to which is the best way to hunt the next few yards, the next mile will take care of itself. The covert will begin to reveal its inner secrets. The bits and pieces will fit together and it will

The dappled light-and-dark coloration of the ruffed grouse is an effective camouflage. Hunters usually see grouse only after they flush. *Photo by T. Martinson.*

soon become obvious that there is only one "best" way to hunt a particular stretch of woodland. Stray from that course, once it's found, and you'll be walking past grouse that remain hidden, flush beyond shotgun range, or worse, depart with a thunderclap from the wrong side of the right tree. There is more strategy involved in getting to know a covert than just being able to locate the right combinations of habitat.

The first grouse that flushes from you in an unfamiliar covert will often reveal the routine that other grouse in the same covert are probably following at that particular time of day and season of the year. The first clue can be found at ground zero, the epicenter of the bird's explosion. Why was the grouse there in the first place? Eating possibly, or sunning in a sheltered spot, or traveling on foot from Point A to Point B with a definite purpose. Grouse are never where they are just for the hell of it. There's always a reason. Look around for obvious food sources. (Be careful! There may be other grouse nearby.)

If you bagged this first bird, check the contents of the crop to determine whether there's a match-up with the wild foods in the immediate area. A lack of a match-up, or an empty crop, means that the bird was there for other reasons. But if the crop spills out a handful of dogwood berries and you're standing up to your ears in dogwood bushes, it's time to get very serious about how you take your next step.

The direction in which a grouse flies can provide another clue to a new covert's hidden mysteries. Short, low-to-the-ground flights don't count; all that these tell you, I think, is that a grouse succumbed to an urge to add some distance to your closeness. But those high, soaring flushes—the kind that start off in one direction but then curve into a sky-ripping arc towards distant cover—are the work of grouse intent upon getting back to a specific, oft-used hideaway. Such information, this revealing of secrets, is so valuable that missing said grouse can almost be counted as a plus when you're hunting a new covert. Keep your eye on Ruff as long as you can.

I possess, in the figurative sense, a really sweet covert on state-owned land. It contains grouse so predictable in their flight patterns that a fellow could lay down hard-earned money and win ninety-five percent of the time. I hunt the place accordingly, by following that special corridor only I know exists. This covert, which I've aptly named Wall Street, is a square, twenty-acre sloping patch of hawthorn and poplar trees banked with dense clusters of viburnum bushes, and it's surrounded on three sides by evergreen forest. A rutted dirt road, where I park the car, flanks the remaining side. I've flushed at least

150 grouse here over the last decade, probably more. Nearly every one of these gallant birds, repeaters no doubt included, has headed towards one or the other of the two lower corners. Survivors, of which there have been many, disappear into the depths of evergreens, where I seldom have been able to manage follow-up flushes.

If I were to hunt this covert in the way it most obviously presents itself to the roadside observer – that is, straight in and then head for the thick stuff – I'd be making a real mistake in tactics. Grouse that heard the tinkle of my dog's bell or the sounds I might make coming in from the road would be inclined to retreat on foot to the inner sanctum of the evergreens, before I could get close enough to flush them.

No, although I actually *do* want the grouse to hear me eventually, I don't want my presence detected until I've entered the lower evergreen hideaway by a roundabout way, a logging road that follows the southern edge of the covert. Doing this places me in a very strategic position: between the upland feeding/sunning area and the gloomy evergreens towards which the grouse inevitably flush. *Now* I want the grouse to hear me; I whistle the dog onward and shout unneeded encouragements. Ruffed grouse on the sloping hillside could then, if they were so inclined, escape me by flushing wildly in directions other than the one by which I begin my approach. But they don't. They hunker down amidst the shadows of certain bushes or trees (there are fewer than a dozen key places here where grouse flush, but I never know which ones are temporarily loaded) and await the coming of my dog or me. We do get there eventually, via a route that approximates an "S."

Nearly every grouse that I flush, by approaching from this roadward direction, flies high and around me towards the evergreens at my rear. That's maybe an extra two seconds of airborne time within shotgun range, an advantage that has annually permitted me to convert several of the world's finest gamebirds into some of the best gourmet meals.

How To Locate New Coverts

I have neither the time for all the grouse hunting I'd like to do, nor sufficient square miles of grouse covert in which to do it. Oh, the problems of life! Like the rest of us, I devise various schemes by which a few extra hours afield can be wrangled here and there. For example, one year I managed to schedule a couple weeks' vacation in late October on the grounds that "the barn windows needed fixing." (My wife had hoped for a trip someplace, anyplace, earlier in summer.) This autumn arrangement worked out neatly. I'd fix one window, then go hunting. Next day, same thing, with perhaps slightly less emphasis on barn work and a little more on outdoor recreation. ("Gee, Peg, I can't work *all* the time!") By the end of that great vacation, I had more grouse bagged than windows fixed, and I had outlined a general plan for milking the barn project for the next five years.

Now, if only we could be that well-organized in building up an itinerary of places to hunt, we'd almost have it made. Like the rest of us, I keep losing grouse coverts. Some fall prey to the advancing bulldozers, while others simply creep past the prime stages of grouse habitat and lose their value as huntable places. The rate of attrition is so great that if I didn't do something about it, I'd eventually have nothing better to do in my spare time than fix barn windows. Consequently, I've worked out a method for locating new grouse coverts, and it seems to work. This is one thing I get serious about.

Keep A List I offer this little piece of advice as the keystone to any plan you might develop for keeping ahead of the combined ravages of bulldozers and time on your grouse hunting endeavors. In my wallet, I have a dog-eared slip of paper upon which are listed some fifty-odd parcels of hunting territory, most of which contain grouse. Now, I can't remember all those places from year to year, at least not without a great deal of effort. The list has become a catch-all record of casual invitations, roadside observations, fragments of conversation overheard at Ruffed Grouse Society banquets, and so on. When I get a few spare hours to go hunting, a quick glance at my list serves as an instant reminder and I don't have to waste time thinking. I just go hunting.

The Property Tax Office Most of the country around where I do much of my grouse hunting is not posted; and in a way, this is bad, not good. I like to know whose land I'm on, and I don't want to be there without permission. It's better to read the owner's name off a posted sign (so I know whom to ask for permission) than be approached by an irate landowner who tells me to hit the road long before I have a chance to tell him what a nice guy I am.

Promising-looking patches of game cover that aren't posted may appear to be the property of nearby farms or rural homes; inquiries at these residences often prove otherwise. Sometimes it seems that no one really knows who owns what, or where. The trend towards dispersed land ownership began in the thirties, with the breakup of small farms. Nowadays, the actual owners may live miles or even several states away.

I have discovered a convenient source of landowner information that not only identifies the owner, but provides his or her address, the number of acres owned, and the boundaries of the property. A similar gold mine of information can also be found near where you hunt. I'm sure of this because I'm talking about the property tax office. (It's usually located at the town clerk's office, and sometimes at the county seat.)

Here you will find outlined, on carefully drawn maps, all the tracts and parcels of land that fall under the jurisdiction of the local tax collector. Boundary dimensions will be shown, as well as all other relevant information. Often, the course of streams and other land-marks will also be inscribed as reference points. Copies of these maps can be obtained for your future reference. The charge is usually only a dollar or so.

The tax office can answer a lot of questions before they have to be asked. For example, I discovered from the tax maps that one large abandoned farm now belongs to a distant gas drilling company. I wrote to the company for permission to hunt there and received a favorable reply. Similarly, I found that several large acreages on the tax maps are owned by retired folks who presently have forwarding ad-dresses in Miami, Phoenix, and so on. My letters and phone calls have, so far, always resulted in permission to advance my grouse hunting ambitions.

Be prepared for an occasional surprise. The world appears differ-ent on a tax map than from the roadside. Whereas backroads in many rural areas are fronted with private homes, cottages, and posted signs, the large blocks of forested areas behind them are often the property of someone else. You may also discover that many farmers and other landowners possess large tracts of land that are not located near their homes.

Knowledge of who owns the land you want to hunt is obviously no guarantee that permission will be granted. However, it has been my experience that if you can intelligently discuss his acreage and boundaries, the landowner will be more likely to grant permission. You will have demonstrated your willingness to make an effort for the sake of your sport, and that speaks well for you.

Roadside Prospecting   The worst time to go roadside prospecting for grouse coverts is in October and November, when you should instead be inside a woods doing what comes naturally. Summer isn't much better; the foliage is so thick then that you can't see the forest for the trees. Late winter, however, is an especially good time to look for fall hunting coverts, because the tangles of underbrush are down, the trees are barren, and you can view grouse habitat at its weakest link in the yearly cycle. If you can't find the barest essentials, you won't find many grouse there next autumn. Look for conifer cover adjacent to poplars, thornapple, and all the other food shrubs and trees. A trite formula doesn't necessarily produce grouse, but it sure increases your chances.

I also do a lot of roadside prospecting during the spring wild turkey season. At this time of year, male grouse are on their drumming logs, virtually advertising their presence. Although it's not unusual for a drumming grouse to answer my roadside attempts at turkey calling, simply blowing the car horn produces the same effect. I have also attempted slapping my stomach to simulate drumming (and truly believe that the occasional response has been a result of it), but usually I just produce a belch.

Turkey hunters often volunteer that they've heard drumming here or there. I know they sometimes lie to me about the gobbler turkeys they've heard (or imagined), but their information on grouse . . . well, I just nonchalantly tuck that away for future reference.

Use Geological Survey Maps I know that there has been a lot written about this subject in the major outdoor magazines, but most of us still

Male ruffed grouse drum most often in spring and in the autumn. The hollow thudding sound of their wings can betray the location of hidden grouse coverts. *Photo by T. Martinson.*

think that the use of these maps applies only to elk hunting out West. Actually, the Survey maps are far more useful to the grouse hunter than are some two-year-old bird dogs (often by a long shot).

I use the 1:25,000 ratio maps, which show extreme detail right down to the point of portraying houses and barns as small black rectangles, and orchards as rows of green dots.

I've found forest streams that I didn't know existed and island refuges in alder swamps that have provided near-miraculous woodcock hunting. Survey maps reveal the world that hides behind the horizon, as seen from the roadside.

Most Survey maps are at least slightly outdated. That is, the folks who draw them have not always been able to keep up with the conversion of small farmlots into overgrown woodlands. (On these maps, the color green means forest, while white means cleared land.) If you find an area that appears, from a roadside, to be overgrown, yet the map shows white there check out the place for potential grouse cover. Even though the map indicates cleared farmland back in, say, 1950, you'll likely find poplar and hawthorn (and grouse) in place of corn-fields and pasture.

Investigate State-Owned Lands The ways in which state-owned lands are managed for timber and wildlife vary considerably from one region to the next, but there often exists a common denominator that makes these lands worth investigating for grouse coverts. This commonality is the Depression. Many small farms were vacated in the 1930s. After the last cow had been sold and the milk bucket scrubbed and hung to dry for the last time, many a hard-pressed farmer sold or forfeited his property to the state. Most of this happened a half century ago. A mature hardwood forest can grow in that length of time where corn was once sown, but only if seedlings are planted to save time. Not given this advantage, many farmlands were invaded by dogwood and viburnum and by the ranks of fast-growing poplars and evergreens. I have found many empty house foundations and rusted pails on state-owned land, right smack-dab in the middle of some of the world's best grouse coverts. I have even been known to remove my hat in silent salute to the departed folks, particularly if the sun has set and I am late in returning to the warmth and light of the car at roadside.

Even where pine plantations are cultivated on state land in neat even rows of what many wildlife biologists call "green deserts," good grouse hunting can often be found along the brushy perimeters. Ironically, many hunters avoid hunting state lands, believing either that (1)

Dogwood and viburnum bushes often are the first sources of grouse food to grow on abandoned lands.

everyone else hunts there already, or (2) a *real* hunter doesn't need help from the state to find game. I say, take it or leave it. Taking this a step farther, I say that if you want to find classic grouse cover, visit your nearest state conservation agency and check their maps. You may even discover lands unknown to the unquestioning hunting public.

Love Thy Landowner "Hello. My name is Dennis Walrod. I live a few roads over from here."

"Yeah?"

"Yep. I've noticed that there's a patch of poplars down across your pasture where I'll bet a fellow could flush a grouse or two, and I was wondering if . . . "

"No partridge down there."

"Well, uh, I'd sure appreciate it if my dog here and I could—"

"What kind of dog is that?"

"She's an English pointer."

"She any good?"

"Well, yeah, sometimes she's the best dog in Chautauqua County, but sometimes—"

"You don't need a dog to hunt partridge. My boy shot one last year all by himself."

"Oh yeah? That's great! Where'd he find it?"

"Behind the house, over past that orchard. Kid was tickled pink that he finally got one. I sorta don't want to let other hunters in there, case the boy wants to try his luck on bird number two someday. Fact, he's out there somewhere now."

"Sure enough, I know what you mean. A boy hunting for grouse doesn't need any competition. Thanks anyway. I'll be on my way." (I turn to go.)

"There's plenty of grouse on Fred Johnson's place, half mile down the road there. We flushed a bunch of 'em last winter cutting wood." (I stop in my tracks—on point!) "Wait here just a second. No, c'mon in. I'll give him a call and tellum you're coming over."

Is this a piece of fiction? A daydream? Or perhaps a parody of how we'd like things to be with landowners? No, none of the above. I've been in such a scene so many times that, although I might not have the dialogue down quite right here, the ending is absolutely true-to-life.

Landowners are real people; nearly all of these people are nice folks. And those who've had the beejeebers scared out of 'em enough times by thundering grouse are at least willing to discuss the subject of grouse hunting, whether they know anything about it or not. People who are familiar with just the explosive ways of grouse tend to have a built-in respect for the grouse hunter. (Either that, or they consider us to be harmless fools.)

Many of my best leads—hot tips that have placed my boots in superb upland grouse cover—have come from landowners. They've steered me towards hidden gems, they've referred me to country neighbors who owned even better coverts, and they've invited me to come back next year "to keep an eye on things." Am I some sort of particularly charming person? No, not by a long shot. Ask my wife. My only credential, as far as most unsuspecting landowners are concerned, is that I am a grouse hunter. In fact, there's one old fellow who knows me by that name only, the Grouse Hunter, and he seems pleased each autumn when I return to his orchards. Another landowner has asked me to please park in his driveway so my car won't get sideswiped on the highway. Of course, the fact that I took this man's son hunting with me a couple of times didn't hurt the situation a bit.

The annual Christmas cards don't do any harm either. And the offer of a shared gamebag—"Thanks just the same"—has never injured my status as a welcome hunter.

You might consider all this to be a polishing of the old apple. Maybe, just sometimes, it is. But would you borrow a neighbor's car without putting gas in his tank? I genuinely appreciate the permission to use landowners' acreages, and in turn I try to be the sort of guy whom you'd let use your car. If these kind people, landowners who really know what they own, also care to tell me where else I can find ruffed grouse, well, I'm always ready to listen.

Self-Denial and the Road to Happiness The most effective way to find new grouse coverts is to make yourself stop hunting the old favorites. Ouch! It hurts to even think about doing something like that. Grouse hunters are as addicted to following last year's routines as they are hooked on autumn itself. We long to visit familiar turf, to pluck cider-plump apples from the very same tree that has been feeding us for years. Our personal coverts are locked into our brains as units of memory no less real than we are. But how did we manage to discover such intriguing and lovely places? We did it by breaking the routine, by taking chances on wasting time and footsteps when we could have been hunting coverts even older and more familiar.

A fellow grouse hunter told me that he and his partner once made a pact. For an entire season, they would limit themselves to only one hunt per covert, regardless of how abundant the grouse were in each covert. Their intent was to get out of a rut, to make themselves forge ahead towards new and different regions.

Their drastic method worked. Several beautiful and richly populated coverts were added to their list of places to hunt *next* year. But even more rewarding, I was told, was their enhanced appreciation of the experiences of grouse hunting. The pact made the trip into each covert an annual event (if only for one year). They knew that a step taken forward would not be repeated and that each flush was a one-time opportunity. They found themselves hunting harder, shooting better, and enjoying their sport more intensely. Of course, the following year they were back in a rut. But it was a new one.

Rating a Covert

Grouse hunting can be so strenuous, so demanding, and yet still be devoid of any promise of a little heft to the gamebag. Sometimes we pause in our tracks, perhaps miles past the last flush, and wonder:

How long should we expect to keep going and still be considered "normal"? Ah, that's a good question, considering that grouse hunters as a group are somewhat abnormal! (Can you think of any other sport, other than horseshoes, where a miss is scored almost as high as a hit?) We wander around the woodlands, flushing an occasional grouse here and there, wondering just as occasionally whether *other* hunters would subject themselves to such physical abuse. The answer, or an indication of it, is shown below. An informal survey, conducted in 1984 by Ken Szabo for the Loyal Order of Dedicated Grouse Hunters newsletter, revealed that most hunters would consider a flush rate of one to two birds an hour to be "good." That's on the average, of course. Your mileage may vary, as the commercials say, for any given day afield.

Flush Rate Per Hour	Season Termed
0.5 or less	Poor
0.5–1.0	Fair
1.0–2.0	Good
2.0–3.0	Very good
3.0 or more	Excellent

I see no reason why a single covert could not also be ranked in this way. You might not agree with these numbers but, be aware, most other grouse hunters would disagree with *your* numbers.

Using the Back Door for a New Perspective

At least once a year, it seems, I get temporarily lost in familiar woods. Well, perhaps not really lost, but sufficiently turned around so that the portion of the covert my eyes now behold seems strange and new. I find these little moments to be oddly thrilling; they provide me with the rare gift of a revealed perspective, a renewed intimacy. What I'm usually seeing is the backside of the same old covert.

My first reaction is apt to be something like, "Wow! Why haven't I hunted *this* great spot before?" An ancient orchard seems suddenly more dignified in its old age, or perhaps a little sunlit clearing in the woodlands acquires the fleeting enchantment of the never-before and never-again. Then this special awareness fades and the next step taken brings me back to the realization that I've been here, in this exact spot many times—but facing in the opposite direction.

I'm a few years too old to have been a member of the "if it feels good, do it" generation, but this doesn't stop me from trying to repeat the circumstances that lead to these enthralling experiences in the autumn woodlands. Simply put, I often break my hunting routine and walk into the same old covert through the back door. I enter where I usually depart, and I exit at the familiar front door.

By doing this, I not only get a chance to inspect the covert from a fresh angle, but the grouse therein seem to sit more tightly, as though confused (has a spell been cast?) by my departure from the norm. It's possible that their earlier encounters with me—the close misses they've survived after my repeated approaches from a different direction—have taught them that predictable danger only arrives from certain quarters. Whatever their logic might be, I've found that the back door often opens to new opportunities in a covert that appears to have gone stagnant. Grouse seem to let me get closer, permitting me to pass through that invisible barrier a few extra feet, before they trip the release and catapult into blurred action.

My bird dog even runs a different pattern when we work a familiar covert in an unfamiliar direction. She typically learns quickly where opportunities are most apt to be found, so I assume that she, or any other good bird dog, will begin taking wasteful shortcuts in familiar cover if a break in the routine doesn't get tossed into a day's hunting. Pure nose—scenting ability—can't really do the whole job for a man/dog hunting team. The dog must truly be hunting all possible cover if those black wet nostrils are to bring her to the right places. By loosing Pup through the back door, you encourage the dog to work a little harder at finding game. I believe that a dog develops a more intimate relationship with a grouse covert than does his or her master; a dog is thus more prone to hit only the high spots, to the exclusion of all others.

The back-door approach is most effective for the hunter who goes afield *without* a dog. Stalking grouse—hunting them in such a careful way that they neither flush too far from the gun nor hold so tightly as to not flush at all—is a sport requiring precision of movement. In a well-known covert, grouse will (more often than not) flush in predictable directions from certain spots where memory has carved an indelible foothold. After a few seasons, a grouse hunter may develop a pattern of hunting a particular covert so rigid that some of his actions border on superstitious ritual. If a grouse happens to flush when you pass the left side of a certain anthill, brother, you will likely veer to the left the very next time that anthill appears in sight. Should a grouse flush once again when you repeat this behavior, you're hooked. For at least the next decade, you will never pass this spot again without following that magic corridor. Only test pilots and major-league base-ball pitchers, besides other grouse hunters, can really understand what we're talking about here. Superstition is born when something works right but without explanation, and only the unlucky would question why.

It's when the rituals *stop* working that it's time for a change. The back-door route opens up new possibilities and shakes the dust off old habits. Try occasionally working some familiar coverts this way, and you will probably discover that the magic corridor has some twists and turns into even better patches of grouse cover—ones you didn't know existed.

5

Grouse Guns and
Other Equipment

I have long been certain that the rank and file of grouse hunters are comprised of rugged individuals who partake of their sport with little regard for the conformity of tradition. When you come right down to it, the average modern grouse hunter carries whichever shotgun he happens to feel comfortable with—or happens to own. Yet I have also harbored the belief that deep in the core of hunterdom there exists a solid cadre of experienced grouse hunters, protectors of the true faith, from whom spring all the traditions, standards, and specifications (make, model, gauge, etc.) of the sport. Don't ask me how I had come to believe such pap. Maybe I read it somewhere. Certainly if such a fountainhead of wisdom did exist, it could be found amidst the dedicated membership of a national ruffed grouse organization. A poll of these members would undoubtedly reveal for us, once and for all, the criteria for selection of the mystical *Right Shotgun*.

As it turns out, such a survey has been performed annually for several years, and the results repeatedly reveal that dedicated grouse hunters have mixed opinions about shotgun preferences. In fact, their opinions are more scrambled than mixed, as you can see below in the data supplied by members of the Loyal Order of Dedicated Grouse Hunters. This organization is now over 2,000 strong, and the 338 brushworn members who turned in their logs following the 1982–83 hunting season—so that all of us could learn the inner secrets of grouse gunnery—are undoubtedly more than just your average nimrods. They're truly dedicated sportsmen. Most of them consider themselves to be Grouse Hunters, rather than mere hunters. They pay membership dues, and they're sufficiently motivated to maintain yearly logs of their hunting activities and equipment preferences. This latter item—equipment preferences—may not seem all that big a deal—but it really is. What we have here is a tap that leads directly into the inner core, the solid cadre of grouse hunterdom. And what we discover in this rarified element is a distinct departure from traditional gun preferences.

The following chart lists the various combinations of shotgun type and gauge in descending order of popularity. Note that the most popular combination (over/under 20 gauge) is used by only 18.3 percent of dedicated grouse hunters—a far cry from a majority! Perhaps even more interesting is the selection of the much-maligned and "unsophisticated" automatic 12 gauge, at second place in the ratings. If

Shotgun Type and Gauge Combinations
Ranked in Order of Popularity

Combination	Preference (%)
Over/under 20 gauge	18.3
Automatic 12 gauge	16.9
Side-by-side 20 gauge	13.3
Automatic 20 gauge	11.8
Side-by-side 12 gauge	9.2
Over/under 12 gauge	8.6
Pump 12 gauge	5.9
Pump 20 gauge	5.6
Automatic 16 gauge	2.4
Pump 16 gauge	2.1
Side-by-side 28 gauge	1.2

this chart indicates nothing else, it tells us that no matter which combination of gun and gauge we personally prefer, the majority of dedicated grouse hunters will disagree with our choice. But then, they too appear as a minority, somewhere on this list.

There's another way of looking at the gunnery data supplied by Loyal Order grouse hunters, and that's with shotgun type and gauge preferences shown separately.

Shotgun Type	Preference (%)
Automatic	31.3
Double	27.9
Over/under	27.1
Pump	13.7

Gauge	Preference (%)
20	49.1
12	40.5
16	9.2
28	1.2

The automatic shotgun is thus exposed as the favorite for grouse hunting, just as it is for virtually every other hunting sport plus skeet and trap shooting. Perhaps we expected the side-by-side shotgun to be the first choice among dedicated grouse hunters. But it isn't. Note, however, that the pump shotgun is in last place. I interpret this to mean that grouse hunters desire the capability of fast shooting, and the pump is truly fast only in the hands of a highly experienced shooter.

From here we go on to a comparison of gauge preferences. Note that although the 12 gauge attracts a hefty 40.5 percent of dedicated grouse hunters, it's in a minority to the total of the others combined. What I think this means is that grouse hunters favor the lighter weight guns in the upland coverts, much more so than do their cousins, in the duck blinds and whitetail woodlands, who tend to sit more and walk less.

What this all comes down to is that there really isn't a "right shotgun" for hunting the ruffed grouse. Each make and model has its own staunch advocates, and for good reasons. Different guns handle and shoot in different ways, but it's we who are doing the hitting and the missing—not the guns.

I personally prefer a side-by-side shotgun, and the one I carry happens to be a little 28 gauge. (The merits of this particular gauge are discussed a few pages later.) What I especially like about a two-burner grouse gun is the instant choice it provides me for the selection of choke. Birds that flush at close range must reckon with the possible

A 20 gauge over/under shotgun, a canvas hunting jacket, and a bird dog that will stand
still when told to do so. And a fallen grouse. These items are first choice among
grouse hunters.

consequences of the more open-bored first barrel. When I miss this
first shot (not if), I get a second chance at longer distances with the
tighter bored second barrel. Besides the capacity for choke selection
and the rapid shooting of two shots, the side-by-side also provides
what I consider to be the advantage of a wide-angled sighting plain. In
shooting position, the hunter's eye sights from a perspective of two
barrels aligned like the two lanes of a highway laid straight across a
desert, meeting at a single point on the distant horizon. A single-

barreled shotgun presents only one angle to the computer in your head; a side-by-side inputs twice as much aiming data.

Grouse gunning is more instinct than thought. There's not much time for swing, lead, and all that other technical stuff. I believe that a side-by-side can be pointed more reflexively and more accurately during the momentary chaos of a grouse's flight than any other type of gun. By me, that is. I'm afflicted with the sorry combination of being right-handed and left-eyed, so I need all the help I can get from the sighting plane of a shotgun.

It would be neither proper nor valid for me to state that a side-by-side is the one gun ruffed grouse hunters should carry. There is temptation here for me to act as though I had a right to make such a recommendation, but I'll resist it. Instead, I'll suggest that you hunt grouse with any type of shotgun that is easy for *you* to carry, sweet to handle, and quick to follow the invisible arc traced by an even quicker grouse. Guns don't kill grouse; people kill grouse.

Best Chokes and Shot Sizes for Grouse

This is a subject worthy of great debate; many debates have already been held well into the wee hours of the morning. Everyone, it seems, has his own idea about the merits of various gun chokes and shot sizes for grouse. Nobody ever wins in these debates, and yet no one ever quits trying. We toss another log on the fire, get another refill so the ice cubes will float again, settle back in our chairs, and resume arguing.

The AYA 28 gauge Model 3A double-barreled shotgun used by the author for grouse hunting.

The reason for the controversy is that each of our opinions is at least a little bit right on target. There's no real right and wrong here. The final judgment rests on how the birds were flying on a particular day—and for that day only.

Coarse shot, such as Nos. 4 and 6, maintain a greater killing energy over longer distances, but their larger size limits the number of pellets that can be loaded in a shot shell. Fine shot, such as Nos. 8 and 9, lose their momentum in flight very rapidly, but (it can be argued) make up for this deficiency in the sheer numbers of these small pellets in the pattern.

When you add the effect of gun choke to these considerations of shot size, the debate takes on new dimensions. "Skeet" or "improved cylinder" bore will throw a load of coarse No. 4 shot all over the map at, say, 35 yards and might leave holes in the pattern big enough for a wild turkey to pass unscathed. On the other hand, a more tightly bored "modified" choke might throw such a dense cluster of No. 8 or No. 9 shot that any grouse with which it connects, at 20 yards or less, is likely to be blown right *off* the map. When this happens, your plans for a gourmet supper can go up in a cloud of feathers.

In either extreme of distance and choke/shot size combination, there's one fact that's always true: We really don't *have* to shoot just because a grouse has flushed. This moot point settles the debate as far as I'm concerned. You can never be the least bit certain whether your choice of choke and shot load is appropriate until the next grouse suddenly bursts into view. Then, a quick decision is required to shoot or hold fire. There is no sense in taking every shot that's offered if there is a risk that either the meat or the sporting ethic might be damaged.

Grouse gunning is far from being an exact science, and yet certain formulas have appeared so often in the popular outdoor magazines (and yes, sometimes, late at night by the fireside), that it's almost tempting to believe in them. For example, one such formula says that winter hunting requires longer shots. This formula is based on the logic that because you can see farther after the leaves have fallen, you'll also have to shoot over greater distances. Consequently, so the theory goes, winter grouse hunters should carry tighter choked guns loaded with coarser shot. Maybe so, but I don't necessarily agree. In fact, I see this whole winter hunting scenario in an entirely different light.

My own version of logic says that the longer shots are more apt to be taken in early autumn rather than in winter! The dense autumn foliage so often conceals a grouse during the first second or so of flight that a truly sporting shot isn't offered until the bird reappears in the open sky at a considerably greater distance. Winter grouse, on the other hand, burst out at just as close range from their snow burrows or off the limbs of evergreens or out from under frozen tangles of undergrowth; and they have no other recourse than to dodge between bare trunks and bush stems. What this means to the hunter is that shots of 30 yards or farther with tighter chokes and coarser pellets are just more feasible, but by choice rather than by chance.

Nothing is certain in grouse hunting, except that things usually don't happen exactly the way you think they will. If they did, you'd eventually find some other way to spend autumn, something with a little grit and challenge to it. Whichever combination of choke and shot size you carry (regardless of the month of the hunting season), it's effective only within the confines of a certain range. Some combinations are suitable only under 20 yards, whereas others can reach out past 40 yards before the pellet pattern gets critically thin. A golfer can carry a whole arsenal of clubs, one for every conceivable lie of the ball. But the grouse hunter can only play his game one way—or two ways, if he's carrying a double-barreled shotgun bored with different chokes. There really aren't any *ideal* combinations of choke and shot size for ruffed grouse. Every flush of a grouse is different from all others; you can only prepare for what you think the average shooting range will be, and then stick literally by your guns and shoot within that range. I have killed many grouse with every shot size from No. 4 to No. 9 (excluding No. 5, of course, which no one seems to manufacture anymore), and I've done it in various combinations of modified, improved cylinder, and skeet-bored choke.

If there is anything even remotely resembling a best combination, it would be something like No. 7½ shot and an improved cylinder choke. The pressures of tradition are upon me to say something like that. Consider, however, that "best" in this case is only a compromise between grouse being too close or too far at the moment of truth. In any case, the true capability of a certain combination can be tested only by shooting at target paper. In chapter 6, I describe a special method that will help you establish the actual effective range for shooting.

The 28 Gauge: Enough Gun for Grouse?

Of course the 28 gauge shotgun can kill grouse. Under the right circumstances (i.e., sawed-off and at close range), this sweet-shooting, graceful little gun could blow the head off a Holstein bull. However, since the average hunter usually doesn't face the need for such a feat, let's consider instead the application of the 28 gauge in the rigors of the grouse coverts of autumn, where said gunner can use all the help he can get.

The basic question then becomes one of whether the lightweight and quick-handling 28 gauge provides an advantage for the grouse hunter, or instead constitutes no more than a prestigious piece of hunting equipment which presumes to separate the "elitist" from the ordinary hunter.

That the 28 gauge shotgun is much easier to carry and handle amidst the grape tangles and thornapples is a point beyond reasonable argument. My Spanish-made, 28 gauge side-by-side weighs barely a feather over five pounds. That's twenty to forty percent less than many of the more popular 12 gauge shotgun models which get lugged afield. This differential can easily be translated into proportionately less fatigue and much faster handling. And for what it's worth, a box of 28 gauge shells takes up a heck of a lot less space in your hunting jacket, leaving more space for dog whistles, bologna sandwiches, and the like.

Many hunters tend to lump the .410 and the 28 gauge in the same belittled, minor-league category. To do so is a mistake, however honest, because the .410 is an entirely different performer. The very narrow bore of the .410 requires that the lighter shot column be uncomfortably elongated to the extent that the resultant ballistics are less than predictable. I definitely do not recommend the .410 for grouse gunning. It truly is a puny gun, suitable only for the destruction of rats and the instruction of children. While we can justifiably admire our purist trout-fishing brethren for their fascination with ultralight tackle and 2-pound test tippets, that same philosophy has no proper place in grouse hunting! We cannot catch-and-release. So when we do take a bird, we want that act to be performed as cleanly as possible.

For that ultimate purpose, the 28 gauge performs remarkably like the 20 gauge, which is an accepted grouse gauge. Statistics supplied by the National Skeet Shooting Association confirm this. Take a look at the following comparison of scores which define "Class A" per 100 clay birds.

According to this performance criteria, there's perhaps five times as much difference between the 12 and 20 gauges as there is between the 20 and the 28 gauges.

The real beauty of the 28 gauge as an upland performer is evident when you first hear that thunder of wings and a grouse hurtles up into sight with all the surprise of a rock through the kitchen window.

Gauge	Shot Weight (ounces)	Score Bracket
.410	½	90.5–93.5
28	¾	92.5–95.5
20	⅞	92.5–96.0
12	1⅛	95.0–97.5

At this moment, you don't have to worry whether your gun is balanced "weight-forward" for proper swing and follow-through. For grouse, you want a poking gun, one that can be smartly brought to your shoulder and stabbed towards the sky before the thunder quits. Most shots at grouse don't require a smooth swing; they're snap shots—taken because seldom is any other offered.

To this purpose, the lightweight 28 gauge is ideal. It moves in your hands with all the ease and agility of a Daisy BB gun, yet carries a wallop at the muzzle end that puts this gauge in direct competition with the 20 gauge skeet and normal low-brass upland loads. In that comparison, the 28 gauge puts out only ⅛ ounce less shot (14 percent fewer pellets) than the 20 gauge, and only the dyed-in-the-wool, big-bore addicts would argue that this is a significant difference.

I first began taking my 28 gauge side-by-side afield for reasons other than hunting. I had a new English pointer bitch that I more or less had broken to wing and shot on pen-raised quail, and I needed a gun along for no real purpose other than to make a noise at the appropriate moments during these training sessions. When the bird season opened and the dog seemed ready for real hunting experiences (under the somewhat controllable conditions offered by tight-sitting woodcock), I carried the 28 gauge into the alder runs. We bagged several of the little brown birds over the course of a few sessions, and I began to realize that the 28 gauge was more than just a loud "popgun." The dog was performing well, too, so we eventually drifted into the adjacent uplands where grouse lurked.

In that first season, I still believed that I was grossly under-gunned and consequently I restricted my shots to only those grouse that were within twenty yards or so. However, the comparative quickness with which the light 28 gauge came up to my shoulder for those close-ranged shots more than compensated for my self-imposed range limitation.

I've carried this same little gun now for several years of grouse hunting. My annual harvest and shooting percentages are the same as for the earlier years of hunting chiefly with 12 gauge bores. I still refrain from taking certain longer shots that could have been easily made with bigger bore guns; but as it turns out, there aren't as many of those kinds of opportunities lost as I thought there would be. At any rate, provided with slightly tighter chokes, the 28 gauge is *almost* as effective as any of the other guns commonly carried into the domain of grouse. And it's a whole lot quicker on the draw than *any* of them.

Sometimes 28 gauge shells are difficult to find in the sporting goods stores, but you can almost always find them in outlets that cater to skeet shooters. The gun itself is enjoying a resurgence of popularity, and there are several models now being made. These include H & R Model 49 (single shot only), Winchester Model 101 (over/under) and Model 21 (side-by-side), Browning Citori (over/under), Remington Model 870 (pump), and Davidson Firearms (side-by-side). The 28 gauge is also offered by AYA, Beretta, Franchi, Krieghoff, Merkel, and Perazzi. If you want one, you can find one. Both guns and shells carry a slight premium in price because of their comparatively low volume on the market, but it's not prohibitive.

I predict that the 28 gauge shotgun will eventually be associated with grouse hunting just as the 10 gauge is with goose hunting. Both are great combinations, much more than adequate, and appropriate to the situations encountered while hunting. The light weight of my 28 gauge frees an arm when necessary, so I can pick thorns out of my ears and burrs off my knees as I attempt to traverse and survive my favorite grouse coverts. When a grouse flushes, I am more apt to be *ON*! that noble bird quickly—and I don't fall down as often as I used to. Moreover, if I still happen to be on that bird when the trigger somehow gets pulled, the pattern and power of the 28 gauge are sufficient to render unto me the choicest of upland gamebirds. Yes, the 28 gauge is enough gun for grouse.

Boots, Brush Chaps, Hunting Vests, and Other Gear

Hunters of the ruffed grouse tend to dress in a fashion somewhat different from hunters of other game. Once again the faint cry of "elitism!" echoes from the far side of the valley where those vast hordes of other hunters sit on logs or perch in tree stands or squat in blinds complacently waiting for squirrels, deer, or ducks to come to *them*. ("Darnation!" they mutter. "Game ain't movin' today!") When the cold wind begins to carry an icy bite, these hunters hunker down some more, turn their wool collars up and their ear flaps down, and grope for the controls for the electric socks—which means they first have to remove their insulated gloves.

The grouse hunter must dress for action, not just for the shooting end of things but also for the finding and flushing of his very special game. Wading through acres of pricker bushes is nobody's idea of real fun, but we do such things because we have an optimistic faith that there absolutely has to be a grouse in there somewhere! And if not there, then certainly in or around the next patch of evil-looking thorns and tangles. We keep moving, undaunted.

There is no place in grouse hunting for sit-still comfort. We need attire that functions in such ways as to let calories of energy out, not to keep them in. We also need more than the usual amount of protection from the jabs, pokes, pricks, and scrapes that any decent grouse cover is ready to provide. We go to our sport; it doesn't come to us.

Boots There is no such thing as a totally perfect boot for grouse hunters. There are only perfect advertisements for boots. I have yet to find a type or style of boot that will last for more than one season and still be able to fulfill, at a reasonable cost, all the grouse hunter's needs for light weight, warmth, traction, comfort, and dryness. I've destroyed so many pairs of boots in pursuit of this special sport that the costs of licenses, guns, and ammo pale in comparison. My opinion is that the best way to keep boots in good condition is to stay home and watch football on television.

Short of that, we need to be able to find something in the closet by the back door that will at least protect our feet from direct contact with the elements. I'm stating this from the viewpoint of a hunter who has shot the majority of his grouse while standing on feet that were either (1) too hot, (2) too cold, or (3) too wet but nicely warmed by exertion.

Leather boots are the nicest when you initially take them out of the box and try them on. The first few forays afield are always a joy (at least for your feet), and the fact that the boots need to be placed on the radiator or beside the wood stove to dry when you get home always seems to be as unquestionably appropriate as feeding the dog or cleaning the game or running an oilcloth over the gun. You just do it. Applications of extracts of mink, beef, or beeswax forestall the inevitable cracking and general deterioration of leather; but the day always arrives, somewhere around the fiftieth mile, when some of that last puddle you stepped in seeps in between your toes. The way I figure it, if leather were perfect for footwear, a cow's hide would extend all the way down to the bottom of her feet. But no, cows have hooves instead.

Mother Nature knows when to quit using leather. Most of us grouse hunters, however, don't possess this particular insight; so we march off to the coverts with dead animal skin wrapped around our feet. Generally, veteran hunters own two pairs of leather boots: one pair for wearing out and the other pair for drying out.

Rubber boots have a lot going for them, yet many hunters shun their use. For some unknown reason, leather is considered to be classic while rubber is relegated to pedestrian status. Perhaps this situation has something to do with the fact that leather costs more than rubber. Boot manufacturers have long recognized this implied distinction, and for many years have marketed a type of boot that is rubber on the bottom half (where it *really counts*) and leather on the top (where it looks nice). But no one has ever designed a seam between leather and rubber that doesn't leak eventually.

One of the nicest, driest, and most comfortable pair of boots I ever wore into a grouse covert was purchased in a farm supply store. They were 100 percent rubber from top to bottom, just plain farmer's boots. It was pure joy to be able to stomp through logging road puddles without feeling that cold trickle familiar to my toes.

The boots were just a trifle cumbersome and clompy, but they let me go where I really wanted to go. Then one day, a protruding stick caught just right and punctured a small hole in the left boot. I patched it with a bicycle tire kit, but the patch peeled back the next weekend when another stick found its target. Soon tired of favoring one foot, I bought another pair of rubber boots. I tore a hole in the left boot that very weekend and cursed the red gods (whoever they are) that never seem to let me match up left-and-right survivors.

Still, full rubber boots are relatively inexpensive, particularly the plain and simple kinds. Also, the flexibility of rubber permits these boots to be designed with a snug ankle fit that reduces fatigue. This type of fit permits a greater range of foot movement, yet still holds the boots tightly up against the soles of your feet where they belong. Another advantage of rubber is that its softness makes a hobnail sole a more practical alternative to a grooved vibram design.

Inexpensive rubber boots are not usually insulated, but an extra pair of wool socks will easily make up for this deficiency at a fraction of the price you'd otherwise pay for warmth. Felt shoes as liners are another option for warmth in rubber boots. Most hunters have never even heard of felt shoes (and neither have many stores), but they're a great invention and not very expensive. If the outer rubber boots spring a leak, you can save the felt shoes for use with a new pair of boots.

Certain synthetic fabrics are now available in combination with traditional leather and/or rubber boot designs, and some very good recommendations from grouse hunters here and there are beginning to be heard. These boots are rugged, waterproof, and yet are almost as lightweight as a pair of basketball gym shoes. No doubt, styles and types of boots will evolve to the point that a ruffed grouse hunter can select whatever size and color he wants, without having to worry at all about sharp sticks and boggy ground. Perhaps someday someone will invent a boot that holds warmth, repels water, and does not restrict freedom of movement.

Brush Chaps   Brush chaps and brush pants are commonsense solutions to the thorny problem of how to get to the other side of a grouse covert with a minimum of pain. Wading deep into a briar patch is often the only way to effectively spring grouse into flight, but we unnecessarily sacrifice the integrity of our kneecaps by such a maneuver. To remain unpunctured is no shame, regardless of how stalwart or otherwise brave we are as grouse hunters. Sure, hunters of other game may snicker and giggle at our attire, but they don't understand what *real* hunting is. They haven't been where we routinely go.

Nylon chaps, canvas vest, and shooting glasses reduce the amount of human flesh that might otherwise hang from the thorns and barbs of autumn grouse coverts.

Thorns don't just prick and puncture; they also drag, cling, and pull against a grouse hunter's forward motion. Brush chaps and brush pants both protect a hunter's legs and contribute to freedom of movement.

Chaps are worn over ordinary pants. Brush pants already have the "chaps" sewn in place. Both types usually incorporate nylon fabric in one form or another on the front facings. A urethane coating is often applied to the nylon for extra waterproofing. Cordura nylon is quieter than ordinary nylon; it doesn't rustle as much during briar swimming sessions.

Heavy-duty denim workpants technically don't fall into the category of brush pants, but are almost as suitable for rugged use in the grouse coverts. Homemade chaps can be made by cutting the boot ends from a pair of waders or hip boots and adding a short slit up each inseam so they'll fit over other boots.

Vests and Jackets   There was a time, not too many years ago, when it was quite common to buy poorly designed outdoor apparel. Some garments were so bulky and inflexible that they were more appropriate for grizzly bear wrestling than ruffed grouse hunting. Today, a sportsman can easily find what he wants and needs in a vest or a jacket: deep, flapped pockets (and plenty of them), removable and washable gamebags, brush resistance, light weight, and comfort.

Nearly all vests are now made from coarse fabrics similar to canvas, or from sleek nylon. Both types of fabric are highly suited to the grouse hunter's needs during brush-bucking, but neither type is particularly useful for warding off the cold. That's alright; a vest is not meant to perform that function. In fact, vests are meant to lose body heat, not keep it.

Sometimes it's sunny and downright hot during the first few weeks of the autumn grouse season. A light cotton shirt is plenty enough clothing, and a vest is needed then only for the extra pockets it provides for ammunition and other paraphernalia. Later in the season, a wool shirt or sweatshirt can be substituted as needed, and if the clouds slide away from the sun and the temperature rises, these heavier garments can always be stuffed into the vest's gamebag. That's what a vest is for: a place to put things when you have no immediate need for them.

So, shouldn't a full jacket fulfill those same requirements? I maintain that a hunting jacket should be no more than a vest-with-sleeves, as long as these sleeves are loose fitting and offer no resistance to fast shooting. Conventional insulated hunting coats are simply not suitable for grouse gunning. Every time you lift your arms to shoot, you have to lift the combined weight of at least half a box of shells, candy bars, maybe a loaded sandwich, contents of the gamebag, and anything else that happens to be stored in the pockets of such a coat. A properly designed canvas or nylon hunting jacket, however, will have sufficient pleating at shoulder and underarm so that arm movement will be unrestrained. Such a jacket will be a thin outer shell, just the right tool for the job—as is a carpenter's apron or an electrician's belt holster.

Underneath, other apparel can be worn as needed for warmth. I've found that a hooded sweatshirt over a ski sweater is more than adequate for the coldest of days afield. The unused hood bunches up nicely around the back of my neck, and it's there when I need it for full protection for the back of my head. When exertion or a rise in temperature calls for less clothing, I just peel off one of these garments and stuff it in the jacket's gamebag. This is really the only use to which gamebags should be applied. They're for storing clothes, cameras, and dog leashes, but not game. I'll tell you more about this in the chapter on the ruffed grouse as a gourmet meal.

Hats A problem facing the writer of any outdoor how-to-do-it book is that most readers already know which way to spit when the wind is blowing. The people who read a grouse book are obviously grouse hunters. They already know a lot about guns, boots, coats, and the whole bit; but they read on, hoping to pick up a new angle, something fresh and different here and there, something worth trying. I know this, and I've tried to cover every subject as though *it* were the one which might be fresh and new or at least different. One never knows.

Now I come to the old hat subject of hats for grouse hunters. I'm supposed to choose between the standard hunter's short-brimmed Jones cap and the popular long-brimmed baseball-type cap. Each has certain drawbacks and advantages, and each has been championed or chastized by other writers on the basis, I suspect, of what *they* happen to wear.

My problem is that I routinely wear both types of caps. I also occasionally wear a full-brimmed wool felt crusher that wads easily into my hip pocket. All three hats afford me with a certain level of protection from scalp scratches and facial whippings. They keep my head warm, shade my eyes from the sun, and keep the rain off my glasses. Wearing any of these hats provides me with that extra little edge of protection when diving into grouse coverts.

The brim of a hat is a valuable asset until the time to shoot arrives. Still, the value of fluorescent orange merits always wearing a hat.

But hats are also a hindrance to the grouse hunter. Thorns pluck them from our heads every ten minutes—and even more often if we're really hunting hard. The bigger the brim, the worse our chances are for hitting grouse because we need to lift our heads from the gun to even see the birds. So we shoot high and miss. A knitted ski cap is about the best thing available for a snug fit and warmth, but the absence of protective brim or visor strongly offsets these advantages of comfort.

It's really a toss-up with no clear winners. There are, in my opinion, no hunter's hats on the market that are suitable for both the hunting and the shooting. I can't even imagine what the ideal hat for an upland gunner would look like. But it would be blaze orange. That's for certain. In fact, in spite of all the drawbacks a hat can present when the time comes to aim and shoot accurately, the value of blaze orange tips the scales in favor of wearing any style of hat that color.

There is a popular notion that hunters wear blaze orange so they won't be mistaken for game animals. This notion is minimally true, but it's not the main reason. The real benefit of blaze orange is not that it describes *what* you are, but *where* you are. Wearing blaze orange is more a courtesy to other hunters than it is a measure of self-protection. Especially if you are hunting with a partner, you have an obligation to wear a blaze-orange cap that can be easily seen bobbing above the chest-high tangles which so often conceal the colors on a vest or jacket. I have passed up many quick shots at fast-fleeing grouse because, at that instant, I did not know exactly where my partner was located. It's difficult enough to keep track of a fellow hunter who is properly rigged with bright color.

Shooting Glasses Wait! Don't let your eyes flicker past to the next section just because you don't want another lecture. I'm talking here about hunter effectiveness, not safety. Let's recklessly ignore the possible eye injuries that can be caused while traversing a grouse covert. Instead, let's consider whether shooting glasses can improve your grouse hunting.

I never wore glasses afield until about halfway through my hunting career. That's when I began to realize that the lettering on too many road signs appeared fuzzy. I can still tell the difference, without glasses, between a grouse and a big red barn at thirty yards, but I now wear prescription glasses anyway. What a new world they have opened to me in the thorny, scratchy, brambly arena of the upland coverts! Never mind better vision. That was nice, sure, but my most pleasant discovery was how much more comfortably I could face my sport head-on and chin-up. No longer did I need to shuffle sideways, eyes averted and squinting, as I plowed through closely interwoven hawthorn bushes and other obnoxious obstacles where grouse lurk.

Shooting glasses are to the grouse hunter what a face mask is to a scuba diver. In either case, these items enhance entry into a different element. With glasses on, you can more deeply immerse your body and soul into the adventure of grouse hunting without undue fear of scratched corneas.

There are other advantages, too. Yellow-tinted shooting glasses increase visual contrast on somber cloudy days. Dark-tinted and photochromic lenses reduce eyestrain on sunny days. I strongly recommend that every serious grouse hunter wear shooting glasses in one form or another. They work even better than brush chaps.

Other Essential Gear Do you need to hear about compasses? No? Oh, so you're one of those fellows who has a "natural sense of direction," always able to come out on the road exactly where it was departed. No matter how long it takes, right? Welcome to the club. I too am gifted with an uncanny ability to find my way—especially when the sun is shining and the distant farmer's dog keeps barking. Directions sometimes get a little vague when both these beacons quit for the day, but that's no real problem. Getting a little bit lost is often sort of fun. Such a situation temporarily reduces hunting (read "surviving") to its barest elements, and the challenge then is not really to endure and live, but to explore and discover.

That's all fine and dandy for the first fifteen minutes. It's when minutes threaten to grow into hours that a compass qualifies as "essential equipment." There's just no sense at all in getting totally lost, regardless of how short or long it might last. I use my compass primarily as a navigational aid. When I'm hunting in the thick tangles of a grouse covert, I go on automatic pilot. I want to be able to concentrate totally on hunting, to follow only my instincts and intuitions towards the magic place where the next grouse will be flushed. Never mind that half the time I don't know exactly where I am. The compass does. It's right there in my pocket, ready to guide me away from the siren song of a wrong direction.

Gut hooks can be made from wire coat hangers, but BUCK's "Bird Knife" is a classier version of the same tool.

There's another item of equipment, one that doesn't make for pretty reading, but its use is essential for the preservation of gamebird flavor. I'm talking about the ignoble gut hook, a device for removing the intestines of a killed grouse with a minimum of fuss or muss.

There's at least one folding knife on the market that contains such an implement. A gut hook can also be made by bending half-inch "hooks" on both ends of a straight five-inch length of coat hanger wire. The hook on one end provides convenient grip when the other end is poked into the bird's body cavity via the anus. Once a loop of intestine has been caught, the whole package can then be neatly withdrawn and discarded. The beauty of this otherwise foul deed is that the flesh of the bird stays fresh and sweet for a much longer period of time.

There are many hunters who prefer to butcher their gamebirds on the spot—skinning, gutting, cutting, and otherwise rendering their quarry into a one-pound chunk of meat within minutes after it hits the ground. Most grouse hunters, however, are inclined to savor the temporary victory of a fallen bird. They delay processing a grouse until the job can be done more carefully at roadside or on the kitchen shelf. The gut hook, ugly in name, helps insure that the quality of the meat will not be harmed by such delays.

6

How to Shoot Ruffed Grouse

S ometimes ignorance is bliss. A good friend of mine used to be a remarkably successful wingshot. Very seldom did a flushed grouse, pheasant, or any other gamebird escape this Deadeye Dick (yes, we called him that on occasion). He never seemed to miss.

Ironically, Dick shot with terrible form. To watch him shoot, you'd think he'd never hit anything. Dick always brought the gunstock up to somewhere near his shoulder, but never lowered his head to sight along the barrel in classic style. He'd just stand there, open-faced and happy, and *look* straight at his quarry. The gun would somehow go off in the right direction and a gamebird would plummet to the ground. You could bet on it.

The fellows over at the local trap club, many of whom had hunted with Dick and seen his prowess with a shotgun, talked him into shooting a round or two of clay birds. He agreed to give it a try. On the very first attempt, Dick shot an almost perfect score. He was obviously destined for world-class greatness. Very seldom does a beginner at trapshooting break many more than half the birds that Dick did. He was then given advice, coached on shooting form and style, and told that his model of shotgun wasn't, well, quite appropriate for trapshooting. Dick could have walked away from it all and, if he had, would probably still be the best wingshot in Chautauqua County. But he didn't, and he isn't. When that first clay bird puffed into smoke against the summer sky, Dick caught a strange disease that can only be cured by shooting several rounds of trap at least once a week. He was hooked.

Dick went the whole route: he bought the right gun, heeded all the advice—of which there was ample supply—and started putting cheek to wood in accepted shooting style. The only thing that my friend didn't do was keep getting good scores. That next autumn in the uplands, he also started missing real gamebirds on the wing. Gradually the trap scores began to improve, but they never reliably stayed much above better-than-mediocre. If there is a lesson to be learned here, it is a replay of an old standby: If it works, don't fix it.

Originally, Dick had been a talented wingshot who trusted his shooter's reflexes and instincts. Then he got "educated." Misses on the trap field became numbers that had bad connotations. Self-conscious effort replaced a natural and uninhibited shooting style.

Although ruffed grouse *hunting* is a sport that generally requires thought and strategy, the *shooting* of grouse is best done reflexively. There's simply not time enough for much thinking when a ruffed grouse appears and disappears within an instant. They're fast. Yes, I'm aware that the most common error in grouse hunting is shooting too soon; that fact is not disputed here. Indeed, there often is an extra half second or more of flight time within visible shotgun range that is wasted by hasty shooting. But this potential advantage doesn't alter the basic reality of grouse gunning. You still need to point a grouse gun, not aim it.

Ruffed grouse thunder into flight with such furious energy, and are able to disappear from sight so quickly and silently, that the mind reels in protest. A grouse! *Bang!* The hunter is left gasping and blinking while, somewhere up ahead, a vortex of spinning leaves unwinds and settles back to the ground. Often he shoots not once but twice, *Bang! Bang!!*, using the first attempt only to set the stage for serious business, much like a speaker who clears his throat before stepping to the podium.

Good shooting, like public speaking, is as much a matter of mental attitude as it is style or form. Especially in the sport of ruffed

Grouse hunters seldom are presented with an open shot, such as the one illustrated in this mock-up photo. Good grouse shooting is more mental attitude than style or form.

grouse hunting, where misses are more the rule than the exception, there is a need for optimism—or at the least, a benign resignation—if the shooting is ever to be improved.

Grouse hunters and other wingshooters tend to talk themselves out of what might otherwise be superb performances. A grouse flushes, the shooter misses and thinks to himself, "Dumb shooting!" The brain, hearing this, records, "I am a dumb shooter." The hunter may resolve that when the next grouse is flushed; he will make a sincere effort, no matter what, to carefully swing the gun's muzzle along the bird's flight path and on past, in a self-conscious attempt to fulfill the equations of distance and velocity. Again the brain obeys, recording the input and perhaps registering a faint "if you say so." But the next bird goes up unexpectedly, as they all do, and this one dodges and darts along a flight path that provides no opportunity for classic shooting form. Another miss. But just then a second grouse erupts; the startled hunter involuntarily pokes the gun at the bird and kills it. The reaction this time is natural and unfettered by conscious thought.

The human computer that is the hunter's brain always knows where the gun is pointed. Even when the grouse hunter is studiously picking his way through a thicket of briars, that very personal computer in his head is processing tremendously complicated calculations of triangulation and projection relative to the ever-changing position of the gun. If you don't believe this, observe the actions of a milling group of experienced gunners at any trap or skeet club as they walk, armed with enough firepower to take a small Pacific island, from clubhouse to the shooting range. Watch the muzzles of their guns weave a careful ballet of avoidances. No one ever lets his gun point at another person, and yet the whole group has its collective mind on matters other than immediate gun safety.

Two Reasons for Poor Shooting

The combination of brain and body is capable of feats of far greater coordination than we tend to credit it. Primitive man was able to kill game with stone, spear, and arrow with extreme accuracy. Those who regularly couldn't did not survive, and they were removed from the gene pool from which modern man was ultimately scooped. Today's wingshooter has thus inherited an awesome potential to be deadly accurate with a hand-held weapon. Except for only two reasons, a grouse hunter should be able to kill every bird that remains within visible shotgun range for a little over one second (not that we'd really want to do that, of course).

The first reason is biological. Nerve impulses move more slowly than the electrical signals of wired machinery. Every instant of time, every beat of a wing, is finished before we actually perceive its reality. This fact is easy for grouse hunters to accept; sometimes a grouse can be gone from sight before we have a chance even to twitch a muscle in purposeful reaction. The only hope a wingshooter has of minimizing this inbuilt time lag is literally to shoot into the next instant of the future. You don't shoot *at* a grouse. You shoot at where it's going to be, or at least where you *think* it's going to be.

There is more involved here than just the standard discussion of shotgun ballistics, however. Unlike clay pigeons and most other gamebirds, ruffed grouse usually don't fly in a nicely predictable straight line. They dodge trees and then dart behind them. They'll thunder under the first grape arbor and then perhaps bore a hole in the sky going over the next one. Even in open woodlands, a grouse in flight will suddenly slap its broad fantail sideways into the airstream to veer off at an unexpected angle.

These short-flighted birds have spent millennia perfecting their escape act in encounters with countless hawks and other quick predators. Nature tested the fates and decided that the ruffed grouse survived most predictably when it acted in a most unpredictable manner. The ruffed grouse throws surprise into the face of the human hunter, just as it treats any other predator. And our nerves can't always cope with that surprise. Signals flicker in haste along neuron paths, but often fail the classic shotgunner's need for proper swing and follow-through.

The instinctive wingshooter, however, has a distinct advantage. For him, there are no vectors of shot charge and bird speed to be mentally calculated when a grouse is flushed. For an instant even the gun itself seems to be forgotten. Only the hunter's eye and the bird exist. The mind perceives and then *becomes* the quarry, flying with wings and anticipating changes in direction.

There are clues, provided in split-second installments. Perhaps a thick hemlock looms ahead; a single wingbeat is dropped from the drum roll, and the fantail begins to tilt one way or the other. The gun's muzzle quickly points towards the now foreseeable future and explodes with a violence that the instinctive shooter hardly even feels or hears. At that instant, if the grouse veers as expected into the sphere of that same future, it will die there. One never knows for certain, though, exactly what a grouse will do. With experience the hunter can begin making better guesses. But over the long haul, I believe that even a computer-controlled robot, armed with a shotgun but handicapped with a slow-fused human-style nervous system, would miss more than an occasional grouse.

The second reason for missed shots at ruffed grouse is strictly a matter of the mind. We try too hard. We don't trust our natural reflexes, and we *think* too much about correcting our mistakes. Wing-shooting becomes more and more mechanical as we try to isolate (and blame) some technical flaw in style or form. But hand us a crumpled piece of paper or a flyswatter and we can hit the wastebasket or kill a fly with relaxed, deadly accuracy. There have been times, honest, when my grouse shooting was so poor that I would have stood a better chance by throwing rocks rather that birdshot.

When the situation gets that desperate, and we've all been there at one time or another, there's need for a reevaluation. Grouse hunting is properly a sport, not a game with numbers. When there's no "score" being kept, there is apt to be much less concern about performance. If we agonize over the last easy miss, we set ourselves up for a tense encounter when the next grouse goes up and away. Then we either freeze in our boots or swing the gun wildly in a frantic attempt to *do it right this time*! But we usually do it wrong under these circumstances.

Consider the fact that the average grouse hunter kills only about one out of three grouse that offer a reasonable shot. Misses are the rule, not the exception in grouse hunting. Ironically, the less a hunter worries about shooting grouse, the more birds he will likely bag. Look at it this way. At forty miles per hour, which is close to the average measured flushing speed, a grouse covers nearly twenty yards in one short second. There literally isn't time enough for both worrying *and* shooting!

Straight Shooting

I'll bet that every grouse hunter still remembers the first grouse he ever shot. Memories of time and place come quickly into focus, and the details of the flush itself can easily be replayed in slow-motion recall. Most of us felt suddenly very lucky when that first grouse fell, because (admit it) we were probably shooting from the hip. That's the way it so often happens for the neophyte hunter. A grouse flushes, the gun suddenly gains about seventy extra pounds, and the only way a shot can possibly be taken is from the hip (or so it seems at the time).

There are several different ways in which instinctive point shooting can be applied to grouse gunning, but hip shooting isn't one of them. Even though it may work every once in a while, there's no excuse for carrying this bad habit into a grouse covert. A gun can be most accurately pointed/aimed/stabbed/poked, or however you want to do it, if it has first been brought closely parallel to the hunter's line of sight. This way, the direction indicated by the gun barrel becomes a part of the sight picture, and fewer nerve messages need to be interpreted and computed for the sake of accuracy.

The time lost in bringing the gun up to the shoulder is more than recouped by the advantages of having achieved good shooting position. Don't get the wrong idea; it *is* possible to become an adept trick shooter if enough time is spent practicing oddball positions. The very best can get jobs with traveling circuses. The rest eventually end up missing more than their fair share of gamebirds and look silly doing it.

There are three separate steps involved in the proper firing of a shotgun. They are (1) mounting the gun, (2) swinging gun and body towards the target, and (3) deciding exactly when and where to shoot. In most wingshooting sports, plus trap and skeet, there's usually plenty of time to perform each of these steps very carefully. In fact, one of the faults that can arise from having too much time to shoot, "riding" the bird, is an erratic swing of the muzzle.

Ruffed grouse hunters don't have the luxury of ample shooting time. We're lucky if there's barely enough time to track a grouse for one brief flickering instant. The three steps of firing a shotgun are no less important for grouse hunting, but they should overlap into one fluid movement. Yet, it's essential to the development of an effective grouse gunning style to visualize all three steps as being separate entities. I'll explain.

Grouse use the element of surprise as their primary escape tactic. The booming roar of wings is usually heard by the hunter before the bird is actually seen. The hunter's natural reaction to this first blast of thunder is to hesitate, perhaps even cringe. I maintain that you need to use the sound of a grouse flushing as an essential call to action. You hear, you move—right now! Valuable fractions of that first second can be saved if the movement of gunstock to shoulder begins the instant that grouse wings are heard. To do so feels unnatural at first, but the action soon becomes habit—a good one.

The second step involves swinging gun and body towards the roar that, by this time, has materialized as a grouse in furious flight. Doing this is no easy feat, under circumstances commonly encountered in grouse coverts. There are many dented tree trunks here and there, providing evidence of grouse hunters thwarted in their attempts to bring a shotgun around in the bird's direction. Branches

The flush of a ruffed grouse is just as difficult to follow with a camera as it is with a gun. Grouse in flight always appear as a blurred image. *Photo by T. Martinson.*

cling, thorns tug, and suddenly the simple act of maneuvering a shot-gun becomes a contortionist's nightmare. My own tactic in thick cover is to carry the gun so that the barrel is always close to my face. I try to never let a branch or vine get between me and the gun. When I stoop, the gun goes with me; and when I straighten up, so does the gun. What I am trying to achieve by doing this is a swift and unhampered mounting of the gun (step one) as I turn amidst the clinging branches towards a flushed grouse (step two).

Grouse seldom flush from straight ahead. They usually lurk in the shadows until the hunter has passed or has turned in a different direction. If you can combine bringing the gun up with a swift turning of your body in the direction of the grouse, you stand a better chance of achieving a very special coordination of mind and gun. This is very important to the grouse hunter.

Each shot taken at grouse is usually done from a position that is slightly different from all previous shots. Shooters whose reflexes are sharpened only by the predictable flights of clay pigeons, straight-away pheasants, or decoyed ducks, will have much difficulty coping with the odd angles and turns of a grouse in flight. By involving hearing, vision, and the physical movement of gun and body in one coordinated response to a grouse flush, an unlocking of uninhibited shooter's reflexes is more likely to occur.

This very nicely sets the stage for the third step, that transcendental moment of deciding when, where (and whether) to shoot. If unrestrained by our self-doubt, the gun's muzzle will more accurately continue to track the target. The momentum is there; we need only to let it happen. Even if at this instant the grouse should quickly twist towards a new direction, the shooter's nerves are now geared to better accommodate that change.

Your personal shooting technique—whether it involves swinging through from behind, establishing an artificial lead, or poking a shot pattern straightaway into the bird's flight path—is good gunning style only if it works at least a third of the time. That's the average success ratio on ruffed grouse. However, if style is getting in the way of good performance, try shooting totally instinctively for a while. Give your natural reflexes a chance to show what they can achieve. When the next grouse goes up in an exuberant display of winged energy, discard negative thought of hit-or-miss, of numbers, of success-or-failure. Just *shoot the bird*!

As the gun comes up and you assume shooting position, put a clear thought into your mind as to exactly what you want to happen. Create a visual image of the shot pellets erupting from the gun's muzzle in the direction you want them to go. Refrain from making any conscious effort to correct or override your shooter's instincts. Then pull the trigger. If you miss, forget the missing. Don't make a judgment of failure.

The first time I tried this technique, I killed three consecutive grouse with three shots. It was easy! Then I started thinking about how great I was doing. That was a mistake. The fourth ruffed grouse that flushed was saved by my desire to keep the string going. I missed it, wasn't even close. A few days later, though, I killed two more grouse back-to-back, and I began to be concerned about this seemingly awesome ability that I had released. I even questioned, during one brief but golden moment of self-congratulation, whether I should keep the technique a secret—for the purpose of game conservation, of course.

Then something strange happened. Strange yet familiar. I resumed missing grouse, not just some of the time but most of the time. I was rescued from an unwanted glut of bird carcasses by the wily grouse and perhaps by my own subconscious feelings. I don't know which for certain, but I really don't care.

Any wild flush of a grouse is a thrilling experience, hit or miss, and it matters little over the long haul of a hunter's career whether the total bag tally is big or small. I recommend this experiment with instinctive shooting to any ruffed grouse hunter who is deep in the rut of a shooter's slump. To make it work, you truly have to ignore for the one brief moment of shooting whether the bird escapes or is dumped. Initially, at least, instinctive shooting is best accomplished with the same carefree attitude of a child who wings a snowball at a stop sign. It's something that you want to let happen, not make happen. Let the grouse hit your shot pattern, not vice versa.

A good field exercise for any upland gunner, instinctive or not, is to practice simulated shooting. This includes all three steps previously described—except that it stops short of actually firing the gun. The quarry may be "tweety" birds, fenceposts, knots in a tree trunk, or anything else that can provide a reference point for quick gun pointing. The idea here is to imagine *grouse!* and to respond as you would in an actual hunting situation. This exercise is a form of programming. It creates something called "muscle memory" and can result in better all-around shooting performance. The typical dedicated grouse hunter might devote upwards of a hundred hours a year to bird hunting, and yet spend only a hundred *seconds* of that time actually shouldering and shooting his gun.

Pot-Shooting, Ground-Sluicing, and Brush-Busting

Every once in a while, especially when you're all geared up with anticipation for the shattering roar of grouse wings, the bird merely vaults up to the nearest branch and perches there in plain sight. This happens most often when a dog has been nosing around nearby for ground scent and the bird doesn't realize that you're there, too.

Opportunities for pot shots are given also to the dogless hunter. So there you stand, knuckles white against the gun, while the grouse unfurls the feathered crest on its head. It peers curiously back at you, eyes glittering nervously. Much soul-searching can take place during the few seconds of this eye-to-eye encounter. Should you shoot? Should you take advantage of this fortuitous event and drop the bird from its perch while there's still a chance?

Or, let's say that you have finally broken through to the far side of a blackberry tangle, and as you pause to catch your breath (and maybe to staunch a flow of blood from your thumb), a grouse flushes nearby and disappears unscathed. But then from the same thicket, you hear a rustling of leaves and look that way. A grouse! Hunkered there amidst the shadows another grouse is seen, frozen immobile by the indecision of whether to flush or hide. Obviously an easy shot; all you have to do is shoot slightly off-center so the meat won't be ruined more than is necessary.

But wait! What about the sporting aspect of ruffed grouse hunting? I've had some hunters tell me that any shot at a ruffed grouse is a sporting shot, and besides (they go on to say), they always eat everything they kill. This explanation is somehow supposed to make everything (even poaching, I suppose) perfectly okay. I don't agree, and most other grouse hunters wouldn't either. Is it acceptable to rob a bank provided all the loot is well spent? In the case of pot-shooting or ground-sluicing, it's the hunter who gets robbed of the very essence of his sport.

Most of the value of a fallen grouse lies in the difficulties involved in bringing the bird to bag. The real treasure there is measured not in pounds of meat, but in the hours spent setting the stage for the rare moment of killing. No, dedicated grouse hunters do not take opportunistic shots at their game. To do so would result in a Pyrrhic victory, in which neither the bird nor the sporting ethic of wingshooting survives.

Brush-busting is a little different, a trifle more forgiveable. In fact, many articles have been written about brush-busting as an essential tactic for grouse hunters. It works like this: You're hunting in thick cover; on the next step forward the sound of blurred wings erupts nearby. The gun swings automatically in that direction, dragging you with it, and for an instant a grouse appears zipping across a patch of blue sky. The gun barrel lines itself up neatly, moves with the bird's momentum, and just as it catches up . . . a pine tree slides into the sight picture and obstructs your view. "No problem!" cries your trigger finger. "Use small No. 9 shot," say the advocates of brush-busting. "More of the pellets will penetrate the foliage." I say, once again, wait! *Hold Fire!*

Thousands of ruffed grouse are successfully dropped from flight each season by brush-busters. Sometimes that's the only kind of shooting offered. The autumn foliage is brilliant and beautiful, but it is also everywhere—and for the grouse hunter, there's just too much of it. Yet there are more thousands of grouse that meet their destiny each year as food for possums and skunks, unaccompanied by wine and wild rice, because brush-busting hunters weren't able to see that they had actually made a hit.

Every grouse hunter knows the feral thrill of an instant kill. There is a puff of feathers, a sudden silent pause before the plunge and the thud of a grouse hitting the ground. The kinetic energy of flight becomes a hunter's possession in that moment. Sadly, the imperfectness of the grouse gunning art doesn't permit every kill to be registered as such. Ruffed grouse have a knack for passing behind trees without appearing as anticipated, on the other side. One never knows for certain after a brush-busting shot whether the failure to find a bird carcass was the result of poor shooting or inadequate searching. Sometimes it's just not possible to stop yourself once the reflexive decision to shoot has been made. Still, that's no excuse for using brush-busting as a routine tactic, especially considering the fact that a grouse, once flushed, can usually be found and flushed again within a few minutes.

Patterning the Grouse Gun

I believe that there have been more articles written about patterning shotguns than there are people alive today who have actually done it. Frankly, the subject is boring. Who cares how many pellets made holes in a 30-inch circle at such-and-such a yardage? It matters somewhere between little to nothing to me whether the choke designation stamped on my shotgun barrel is technically correct. However, what I do seriously want to know is the effective killing range for a given load. If nothing else is learned in these excercises involving taping newsprint onto a cardboard box large enough to ship a cow in, it is that each combination of gun and brand of shotshell load makes a unique pattern of paper holes. That's downright useful information.

A fellow might discover, for example, that his grouse gun shoots a tightly clumped modified pattern with Brand X, and yet throws a more open and evenly spread pattern with Brand Y. You have to really see these possible differences to believe them, I suppose, and the only way to do that is to shoot at paper. Shooting at snowdrifts or clay creek banks is better than nothing, but not by much.

What you really need in order to evaluate the potential of a certain load in a certain gun over a certain range is paper. Two full newspaper pages taped together lengthwise provide enough area for most patternings at normal shooting ranges. Mark the center of this target with a dark five-inch-diameter circle, which closely approximates the vulnerable area of a ruffed grouse's body and also provides a point of aim.

Instead of stepping off a fixed distance such as 20 yards, try the following method for getting results that are more applicable to grouse hunting: Walk a considerable distance away from the target. Then turn and approach it, trying all the while to imagine you are actually hunting grouse. Visualize grouse flushing away from you, towards the target, as you continue walking slowly forward. When the target comes within what you personally consider to be typical range for a decent shot, stop and mark the spot where you're standing. Then carefully but quickly shoot once at the center of the target, aiming or pointing in the same way that you would for a quickly disappearing grouse. After that, pace off the yardage as you go to examine the target.

This exercise, done the way I've suggested, provides you with three bits of information. First, you learn what the actual range is (for you only) for much of your grouse shooting. I'm betting that it's a shorter distance than you thought it would be. The second discovery is the placement of the pattern. It may be located high or low or left or right. Or centered. If you cheat and slowly aim the gun by using the sighting bead or the ventilated rib, you may be even more surprised at where the pattern leaves its holes. Nowhere is it printed on any new gun box, or stamped on any gun barrel, that a shotgun is guaranteed to be sighted-in and accurate by an alignment of the beads or rib. In wingshooting with a shotgun, you aim the whole gun—not just the so-called "sights." Third, you can determine, by a count of the holes in the center of the five-inch-diameter circle, whether you would have cleanly killed a grouse. Yes, one pellet can drop a grouse, but it usually doesn't. I will arbitrarily claim that somewhere between three and six holes in the target's "grouse" indicates a clean kill without excessive damage to the gourmet value of the meat. If you have really peppered the target, it's time to consider a looser choke or perhaps a coarser shot size.

Grouse Reactions to Different Hits

The ruffed grouse is thought by many to be a thin-skinned, lightly feathered creature that will fold wings and crumple to earth if so much as scratched by a single-shot pellet. This simply isn't the way it is. The truth is that grouse hold tenaciously to flight and life.

Nearly fifty percent of a grouse's body weight is dedicated to the powerful muscles of airborne escape, and these throbbing dynamos don't shut down very easily. Only a broken wing or traumatic damage will abruptly knock a grouse from its explosive getaway. Many others no less mortally wounded can continue to fly as though untouched by the sting of pellets. Seconds later, out of sight of the hunter, they fall dead. Others less severely wounded will seek concealment and later die even more ignobly.

We would prefer that all our grouse kills be quick and clean, but the regrettable fact is that probably half of them are not. It's essential to the sport for the hunter to acknowledge this situation. Fortunately, nearly all the grouse in this remaining half can be successfully recovered by the hunter. The bag take can be substantially increased with no corresponding improvement in shooting ability, if the gunner will just take certain actions that extend beyond the point at which the trigger is pulled. He has only to keep an eye on the bird.

The classic escape flight of a wild, healthy grouse begins with the explosive force of rapidly beating wings in a bid for airspeed and altitude. The thunder is brief, usually lasting just past the point of shotgun range. Then a silent glide begins, seemingly as quick and as jagged as a bolt of lightning. Occasionally bursts of wingbeating may be added for maneuvering over the tops of intervening trees. A grouse will not usually alight within sight of the hunter, but will first hurtle well past the first screening wall of foliage. In most instances, total flight distances will seldom exceed 100 yards.

Any change in this classic flight pattern should be interpreted as strong indication that the bird has been hit—*even if you are almost certain that you missed it*. Be alert; keep your eyes on the fleeing bird and watch for any sign of something different. Grouse react to different hits in ways that characterize the nature of their wounds and provide clues to where they can subsequently be found and claimed.

The clues can be very subtle. I remember one "missed" bird in particular for the lesson it taught me in the fallibilities of shotgunning. The flush had been totally unexpected, more so than usual because I had just stepped off the roadside and was in the process of loading my side-by-side when the grouse tore out of the brush from almost at my feet. I hastily closed the gun and fired, but much too far to the left. And that's not all; most of the shot pattern buried itself in the trunk of a hawthorn tree just a few yards from the gun's muzzle. I saw this happen; I knew the shot was off, and I had solid evidence that this one had been an absolutely clean miss (like so many others).

The grouse twisted and darted down through the covert, and then broke up through the canopy of leaves to rocket across a clearing toward a thick stand of hemlock trees. The flight appeared perfectly normal until the very end. Then something odd happened. The grouse braked with the usual flaring of wings and fantail, but it then carefully and slowly flew to a perch in the closest hemlock. The bird made no effort at all to keep its landing site a secret. Confident that I knew exactly where to reflush the bird, I approached the hemlock from a different angle, and with great determination to do some straight shooting this time. But the grouse didn't flush. I circled the tree and found the bird lying on the ground, belly-up and stone-dead.

Later, when I cleaned the grouse for supper, I discovered that a single deformed pellet had penetrated the chest and lungs. The most likely explanation for this chance kill is that the shot pellet had ricocheted off the side of the tree trunk in the direction of the grouse. The strangeness of that final, deliberate descent was a strong clue that the bird was afflicted, but I misinterpreted it under the presumption of having missed.

A grouse's reaction to a hit in the internal organs is usually more pronounced. As internal bleeding saps the bird's strength to remain aloft, a feeble flutter replaces the normally forceful wingbeats, and the typical power glide is omitted. Birds thus injured approach their landing site very carefully, sometimes hovering momentarily in flight before alighting. They are usually found dead in the same spot.

Any hesitation at all, any change in flight at the moment of the shot, is indication of a hit. A few lost feathers is obvious sign only that feathers were clipped; but a pause in the wingbeat, a dropped leg, or even an added burst of airspeed, is almost sure to mean that the grouse has been hit in a vital area. A tumbling, awkward fall from the sky usually is sign either of a broken wing or an injury to the muscles

The reward of diligent search.

used for flying. Oftentimes, when a bird hits the ground unable to fly, it still can run—and run it will, towards thick cover under which it can hide.

A bird dog with a good nose is a valuable asset for locating concealed grouse, but the human hunter conducting a little detective work often can "hunt dead" almost as well. The discovery of a loose feather or two provides a clue to the direction a running bird has taken. Usually it doesn't go very far; my experience is that most wounded grouse will be found within a twenty-yard radius of their fall. I have found grouse in hollow logs, woodchuck holes, under overhanging meadow grasses, and beside fallen branches—but most often near the brushy base of a tree.

A thorough search for a fallen grouse begins at the moment the fact of a hit is recognized. Mark the descent well; don't take your eyes off the bird for even an instant. Pause for a moment to take a clear mental picture of where the grouse fell, then proceed directly there. I usually drop my blaze-orange hat on the ground to mark the suspected spot, and then work outwards from there. Looking for a wounded grouse is two-handed work, so I also set down the gun and begin a meticulous, methodical search. Crippled grouse seldom move once they have hidden, so don't expect your mere presence to stir them into betraying their location. I have often found fallen grouse in places where I had already looked. One time, and I swear this is true, I found a bird deeply burrowed into the grass under my hat.

Towering is another phenomenon that injured grouse sometimes display. It is allegedly caused by a pellet hit to the heart or to the brain; no one seems to know for certain, but the heart-or-brain theory seems credible so it's often printed that way.

I've seen towering only twice. The first time, the grouse soared to a spectacular height and then plunged straight to the ground, dead as a fencepost. The second time was while I was preparing the outline for this book. The grouse flushed, I shot, and the bird immediately began an ascent that took it perhaps seventy yards up into the sky, where it helicoptered in circles for part of a minute before plummeting back to earth. I crashed through the brush to recover it, forming plans as I went as to where and how I could get the bird x-rayed for the sake of resolving the question of heart-or-brain for wingshooters everywhere. When I got there, I found the grouse huddled beside a tree. Then, incredibly, it jumped up and ran. I tried to catch the grouse but couldn't, and finally had to shoot a second time, thereby destroying the evidence. Why the first towering grouse fell dead and the second one was so mobile is still a mystery.

The majority of grouse that are bagged always seem to have one broken wing. There's a tendency among wingshooters to attribute this to their shooting skills, but I believe that most of the time the break occurs when the bird hits the ground. Generally, the fracture is adjacent to the first joint of the wing, right next to the body, where the force of impact would most likely be concentrated. The odds are greatly against a shot pellet so often hitting this one place.

All this may not seem terribly important, but it is to the extent that grouse hunters who misinterpret the fact of a broken wing will develop only a vague understanding of how grouse react to different hits. The actual winging of a grouse in midflight is a rare occasion. If that is the only major injury, the bird will tumble clumsily and yet arrive on the ground with its survival instincts in high gear. The search is apt to be long and frustrating because the bird will be well hidden and able to run when found. If, on the other hand, a hit grouse displays the characteristic signs of internal injuries or drops one or both legs over a prolonged descent, the search will be easier. In such circumstances, the fact of a broken wing is irrelevant.

The need to dispatch wounded grouse is on the ugly side of hunting. We prefer to not even have to think about it, so let's be done with the subject in a hurry. If a prime grouse is worthy of mounting, it can be dispatched with a thrust of a knife blade into the rib cage just under the wing. That's where the vital organs are. Bleeding is surprisingly minimal, and the cut is made in a location that won't show on the finished mount. A grouse that is to be rendered only for eating can be dispatched quickly with a sharp rap to the back of the skull.

In the very last moment of his life, Bonasa unwinds with a violent, shuddering drumroll of wings; it's not unlike the boisterous clamor of bell-and-clapper on an old fashioned wind-up alarm clock. When the sound quiets, the dreamed flush is over and the bird is dead. Many times while searching for a fallen grouse, I've been startled by that sudden rumble from undercover and have known then exactly where to go claim my prize. The death knell of grouse wings is both an exciting and sorrowful sound. The drama we perceive therein is in direct measure to our commitment to sport hunting, our acceptance of frustration in the pursuit of this king of gamebirds, and, of course, ourselves.

7

Stalking Autumn
Grouse, One-on-One

There's a great possibility that the one-on-one hunting of the ruffed grouse is sport hunting in its highest form. All the elements of keen adventure are there too: strategy, endeavor, risk of failure, a promise of reward, and, at day's end, an inner glow achieved from having pitted oneself against an adversary worthy of tomorrow's renewed hopes.

There's also much to be said in favor of hunting grouse with the aid of a bird dog or any other kind of breed that has a bird sense. I own such dogs, and I bring them often into the domain of the ruffed grouse. But the maverick in me is addicted to lone hunting, the kind of adventure where nothing much will happen unless I, the predator, personally shake birds loose from their niches in the wild world.

It's my opinion that a hunter is not truly a grouse hunter until he or she can claim proficiency without having to rely upon a dog to put it all together. Stalking grouse alone, and being able to do it well,

When a hunter kills a grouse without the aid of a dog, it is a personal achievement.

provides the hunter with a special insight into grouse behavior that following behind a dog somehow fails to do. This insight, once gained, can help a fellow more wisely guide his dog towards a better hunting performance. Sure it's true that a dog will often reveal the location of hidden grouse when a lone hunter would have passed by without detecting. Still, the one-on-one grouse hunter develops a more intimate relationship with coverts and his quarry. He better understands the tactics required for preventing grouse from flushing too soon or too late, and he knows above all else (better even than a dog) that there are right as well as wrong ways to enter and hunt a covert.

Hunting Habitat the Right Way

Wherever there's a right way, there's also a wrong way. If a fellow wanted for some perverse reason to avoid flushing grouse, well, he could stride straight through a covert to the other side and then keep right on going (as some young bird dogs do). He'd be careful along the way to avoid coming too close to certain clumps of hawthorns, especially those which happened to be banked enticingly up against the shadows of evergreen trees, and he would definitely chart a course that steered clear of wind-sheltered gullies choked with dogwood and viburnum bushes. If by chance a grouse did happen to lurk somewhere along such a route, the odds are that it would flush unseen or at such an awkward angle to the hunter that an honest shooting opportunity would be lost.

There's much more involved in stalking the ruffed grouse than just bumbling around in thick cover, hoping to find a bird or two. Earlier in this book, I described many of the elements of a grouse covert. One of them was the "loose thread," the magic pathway that connects all the most likely grouse haunts and places the hunter in optimum position for both flushing and shooting. Any fool can flush a ruffed grouse now and then, but the wise hunter strives for good position in anticipation of a flush.

Oftentimes it's impossible to second-guess a grouse; but after a hunter has spent a few hours in a new covert, a pattern usually emerges. Depending on the weather and the times of day and season, grouse will be found most often in certain key areas of a covert—and they'll flush in what become reasonably predictable directions. Whether by design or habit, any hunter possessing enough sense to tie his boots will, on return visits to said new covert, begin threading these hotspots together. The loose thread is found, is pulled, and a wild woodland comes together as a comprehensible and properly huntable place, an entity that he can finally own and call a covert.

Now, of course, if a fellow were to pay attention to what was happening around him, he might realize that the lessons learned in one covert can be logically applied to any other covert similar in size and habitat. Ruffed grouse to a certain extent are territorial creatures; they follow daily routines of roosting, feeding, and resting within the confines of their coverts. Except during the autumn dispersal of the brood, ruffed grouse seldom try anything new. Their conservativeness doesn't prevent them from sometimes flushing in any direction possible on a compass, however.

Near the center of a small covert there's no telling which way a grouse will flush, except that it will usually maneuver to get out of your line of sight as soon as it can. The bird may fly only fifty yards or so and then land in a tree from which it can better observe your progress through the covert. If this grouse is eventually found and flushed a second time, it will then almost certainly fly a greater distance, and in a direction that will take the bird into thicker cover. If you realize this in advance, you will approach for the reflush from an angle that intercepts the obvious direction the bird will take.

Ruffed grouse hunting is often like a game of chess, in which ploy and counter-ploy are alternated until one player wins and the other loses. Best position determines the final outcome. I believe that a grouse always knows its flushing strategy *before* those strong wings churn the air into a visible string of thunderclaps. There are exceptions, I suppose; but I've seen too many grouse intricately thread needles, as they've bolted through small openings in seemingly impenetrable cover, to think otherwise. If a grouse is not restrained from following its chosen path, the hunter will usually not be afforded a chance at an open shot.

Consequently, a grouse hunter should approach a likely flush site in such a way that he puts pressure on the bird to question the merits of the original flight plan. I'm serious about this. In most of my favorite coverts, including those which I use for dog training near home, ruffed grouse almost always flush in certain predictable ways from certain familiar haunts. There are many spots where I can literally "point" a suspected grouse into momentary immobility the same way a good bird dog can. Of course I don't stand there with one paw raised and my tail quivering. Instead, I achieve the same tensed effect by walking briskly past a likely lair until I'm under what I believe to be the favored flight lane. Then I suddenly turn towards where I think the bird might be concealed and begin a slow approach—always with more concern for maintaining shooting position than for determining the exact location of the grouse. I try to keep moving; this seems to discourage the grouse from running for a rear exit, and it gets me closer to the quarry.

If and when a grouse does flush, it will be at shorter range than if I had approached from the side opposite the bird's preferred direction of escape. It's easy to tell when this ploy has been done right, by the way the grouse so often steers a course that veers around me, presenting a crossing shot and perhaps even an extra second in which to take it. You recognize such a flight when you see it; there's a resolute curve traced by the bird as it heads towards where it wanted to go in the first place.

In less familiar coverts, the sport of one-on-one grouse stalking takes on different dimensions, which tend to require a slight modification of tactics. Obviously, if a hunter is neither confident of where the grouse are lurking nor knowledgeable about their probable escape routes, he is working at a distinct disadvantage. Nevertheless, when you're hunting grouse, you're hunting habitat. The trick is to learn to recognize those combinations of habitat which have earlier provided good shooting opportunities in better known coverts and then to hunt the less familiar coverts the same way.

A good example of a habitat combination is found along the ragged edges of abandoned pastures, where they butt up against mature conifer forests. Here you will often see thick growths of blackberry canes, wild fruit trees, poplars, birches, and so on. The actual *species* of vegetation aren't nearly as relevant to your strategy as is their *placement* adjacent to the dense conifers. A grouse flushed from the edge cover will invariably fly towards this inner sanctum. You can bet on it. It has been my experience that, on the first flush, a grouse in this type of edge cover will often fly parallel to the outer edge of the conifers for a short distance before swerving to a perch just inside the tree line. Such a bird provides the hunter with an easy opportunity for a re-flush, if missed.

The lone hunter can successfully hunt this particular combination of habitat by stalking carefully along the outside edge of the conifers. But it's usually more productive to wade partway into the low brushy cover before heading in that same direction. When the end of the line is finally reached, it's a good idea to turn around and then make a pass back through the brushy pasture edge, but this time twenty yards or so farther out from the conifers. The idea here is for the hunter to be constantly placing himself between where the grouse probably are and where they probably want to go. To do otherwise is usually a mistake. If this type of edge cover is first hunted along the open outer edge and the taller woodline edge is saved for last, grouse will be more apt to launch at greater distances from the hunter. In thick cover, a straightaway shot is seldom a good one. The bird is heard, but often is not even glimpsed through the intervening foliage.

Another escape tactic which a grouse will use, if approached incorrectly, is to merely run away from the hunter. The lone hunter seldom if ever observes grouse scuttling down through the underbrush—and consequently assumes that they don't ever do it. But they do. Tracks in the snow are *prima facie* evidence of this tactic; the normal meandering tracks of a foraging grouse will be seen to stretch out to an eight- or nine-inch stride on a fresh trail, that usually ends with the marks of wingtips blasted into the snow. Hearing the distant flush, a poorly positioned hunter may wrongly conclude only that the bird was "spooky" and flushed too soon.

Hunting habitat the right way is a great deal more difficult in larger tracts of monotonous cover, the kind of habitat where vast acreages of relatively unvaried growth stretch far beyond the distance

The woodline between evergreens and adjacent brushy growth is often the best path to follow in a grouse covert.

of a single flush. Such coverts typically consist of poplar or birch forests dotted with conifers here and there. A similar type cover often seen on the abandoned farmlands of the northeastern states is the interwoven mesh of hawthorn trees and berry brambles, pierced at random by stunted conifers and the lonely trunks of dead elms.

Which way do grouse flush in these types of cover? Usually any which way they want to. Hunting such cover can be very frustrating; flushes are numerous and yet provide few shooting opportunities. One way out of this dilemma is to keep track of flushed birds for follow-up and reflushing. The stratagem here, in thick monotonous cover, is to approach the landing site as quickly as possible so that the grouse has little time to rest. Subsequent flushes will be weaker and shorter, thus increasing the chances for more open shots. While this tactic might not seem, at first glance, to be particularly sporting, remember that it's a lot easier to read about than it is to do. Hunter skill and endurance are involved, and the bird more often than not eventually eludes its thorn-scratched pursuer.

Any break or departure from monotonous cover in a large covert should be approached cautiously. Fencerows, gullies, clearings, creekbanks, and any other abrupt changes in the features of the land are usually hosts to a greater variety of plant life. In other words, small pockets of "edge" cover will be found in such places. And so will grouse. Such areas also provide better opportunities for the planning of the approach, and for more open shooting. Even seemingly minor interruptions in cover, created by rock piles or the occasional wind-felled tree, are worthy of your close attention.

Oftentimes the most productive route through any type of grouse covert is one that a casual hiker or bird-watcher automatically avoids. The one-on-one grouse hunter has to work hard at doing his own bird-dogging. This is not to imply that the hunter should always plunge ahead into the thickest tangles, believing that there's no gain without pain. More grouse will be flushed this way, but the shots fired will be few and far between, and awkwardly done. Some measure of compromise is required. Forays into very thick cover should be brief and tentative—and only for specific reasons. There should be a game plan; otherwise, mindless wandering will displace purposeful stalking.

Getting Ruffed Grouse to Flush

The ruffed grouse is a master of deception. His first line of defense against predation is the wearing of colors arrayed in an effective camouflage. Held in hand, a grouse is seen to be elegantly plumaged in striking variations of brown, silver, white, and black. At a distance, live and hiding, the grouse is glimpsed only as a shadow or not at all.

The second line of defense is the bird's talent for remaining absolutely motionless in the face of impending danger. Until it perceives the threat as unavoidable, *Bonasa umbellus* plays a waiting game. Flushing is reserved as a last resort. The passing hunter can be easily deceived into believing that the surrounding uplands are devoid of game. Even if he senses that the cover is good and that there should be a grouse here or there, the hunter can be certain of only what he can see and hear.

A dog, however, can smell a grouse and then betray its hiding place. I have learned a great deal from bird dogs, about where grouse hide and what is required to flush them out into the open. Of course, a bird pointed at short range is influenced by the dog's staring pres-

A grouse will not flush until the threat presented by an approaching hunter is perceived to be unavoidable. *Photo by T. Martinson*

ence, and what I have learned in this situation is not totally applicable to this chapter about one-on-one grouse hunting. It has been the long-range points, the ones in which the bird could not possibly have known about the dog, that have presented me with opportunities to analyze just what it is that finally makes a ruffed grouse flush.

When you wade into a thicket in front of a pointing dog, knowing that a grouse is lurking there somewhere (maybe underfoot or twenty yards or so farther into the tangled foliage), you tend to be self-conscious about every move you make. If ten seconds pass and a bird doesn't flush, excitement turns to tension. A new silence begins, swelling to an almost unendurable roar in the ears. After thirty seconds, the dog's integrity becomes questionable. ("Was it another damn rabbit?") But when you look back at the temporarily maligned dog and see bulging eyes in a quivering body, the tail so stiff it probably hurts to hold it that way, you return to the business at hand with a renewed confidence.

Woodcock are easy to flush; all a hunter has to do when one of the little brown birds has been pointed is to stand still and wait for it to lose patience. Using this same tactic on ruffed grouse usually doesn't work. A securely hidden grouse will wait as long as you will. I have come to believe that there are only three reasons why grouse will flush from concealment on the ground.

1. The grouse thinks you can see it.
2. The direction you are following will take you straight to the bird.
3. The grouse detects what its instincts interpret as a momentary lapse in your attention to stalking.

Let's return now to find that grouse hidden somewhere way out in front of a dog still on point. But let's forget the dog; we'll pretend that we're hunting alone, trying to find grouse without the knowledge that one is already nearby and waiting.

Move onward in much the same controlled fashion as you would search for a lost glove. Briefly head straight towards any bush or tangle that might conceal a grouse, then change direction and seek a new objective. Your eyes should seek not grouse, but grouse ground cover.

Much has been claimed about the merits of zigzagging and stop-and-start walking to flush grouse, but I believe these techniques are effective only when they happen to be meshed with the realities of a grouse's own expectations. For example, you can zigzag all you want to through a covert, but if the directions of those little zigs or zags aren't aimed at specific objectives, fewer grouse will be flushed. Similarly, stop-and-start walking is generally a waste of time, unless it's done with the likelihood of coinciding with a grouse in your direct line of sight. A pause associated with eye contact, imagined or real, will trigger a grouse explosion more quickly than any other maneuver. If the hunter purposefully stalks every likely grouse haunt in such a way that birds are tricked into flushing, he will, in actuality, be zigzagging and stopping occasionally. Such actions match those of a natural predator and are thus more effective.

There have been many, many times when I have finally given up on finding a grouse that's been pointed at long distance. I've talked myself into believing that the bird had flushed before I arrived. The intensity of my stalk begins to dim. The gun drifts down from port arms position; I turn to walk back to the dog and *Whrrr!*, a grouse tears up through the undercover and is gone. Grouse often take advantage of quitters. When they've been pressured and then detect a lapse in the hunter's concentration, they blast off for safer territory.

An upland hunter can improve his flushing skills by being more aware of what he is doing at the moment a grouse is successfully launched. Each hunter moves through the woodlands in ways that are different from all other hunters, and I believe this difference accounts for why some hunters consistently see more grouse. They manage to place themselves in the right positions more often. Proper grouse stalking technique is hard, physical work; there are no shortcuts. To make sure that all such effort remains fun and rewarding, the dogless hunter should set a pace that's both relaxed and ready for action. The mind should be cleared of all concern with the mundane matters of daily life so that truly important decisions—such as which side of a bush most likely harbors a grouse—can be made.

Preventing Grouse from Flushing Wild

A small percentage of the time, grouse will flush from way beyond effective shotgun range. They seem more inclined to behave this way on windy days, and I suppose that there are other valid reasons why grouse are a trifle spookier on some days than on others. So am I. Nevertheless, I consider wild flushing to be more a response to hunter technique than anything else. If the manner and direction in which a hunter approaches does not mildly intimidate grouse into seeking nearby concealment (rather than risking full-blown flushes), then wild flushing is what will happen.

The idea here is to determine why the standard techniques aren't working, and to then modify them as needed to make grouse sit more tightly.

Wild flushing on windy days is caused, I believe, by the fact that the grouse's sense of hearing is impaired by the continuous rattle of dry leaves and the sighing of overhead branches. The bird can no longer detect the footfalls of unseen predators. Or, the bird may be able to hear an occasional footstep of an approaching hunter, but not be able to reliably determine the location from which those sounds are coming. In either case, grouse react more quickly to any indication that something is amiss.

Ironically, the best way to get closer to spooky grouse is to let them know you're coming. If grouse can hear you to the extent that they can plot your coordinates at any time, they apparently feel more secure about staying put. Then grouse will wait to determine whether your presence actually represents a danger to them. This means that a certain minimum level of noise-making is required on the part of the hunter. For the whistle-toting handler of a bell-wearing dog, this is no problem at all. However, the lone hunter may feel a little silly humming a happy tune as he struggles with the harsh realities of an upland covert. The best compromise is to stop trying to be quiet; just go ahead and let twigs snap underfoot. Don't try to pussyfoot the thunder bird.

There are many veteran grouse hunters who would argue against the use of noise, claiming instead that the stealthy approach will get a hunter closer to his game. They have a point, but only some of the time. I agree that a hunter should be discreet when first approaching a covert. Otherwise, birds that may be foraging along the covert's edge will be motivated to calmly walk back into the deeper recesses where they're not apt to be found and flushed. Purposeful noisemaking should be withheld until the covert has been entered.

If a hunter were to confide that he was consistently having a problem with grouse flushing wild, wind or no wind, I think I'd advise the fellow to pick up the pace a little, to move more boldly through his coverts. I believe that grouse instinctively abhor sneakiness in the human hunter. Prowling signifies a predator; the grouse senses it and leaves, asking no further questions. But the sight of a briskly walking, brush-busting hunter initially represents no more obvious danger to a grouse than would a passing deer or Farmer Jones on his way to the woodlot. Of course, I doubt very much that the ruffed grouse has intelligence sufficient to detect the difference between a hunter and a farmer, or possibly even between a human and a deer. But I do believe that the tightly coiled mainspring of a ruffed grouse's survival instinct is well geared to recognizing the motions of predators in any form.

Following-up for Reflushes

For the one-on-one grouse hunter, the opportunity for reflushing is a bonus that pays off in the form of guaranteed excitement. The majority of ruffed grouse seldom fly more than a hundred yards or so after the initial flush. Although that distance seems greater in a brambly upland covert than it does on a football field, the good chances of a reflush are worthy of follow-up by the hunter.

There are certain aspects of reflushing so different from normal you-gotta-find-'em-first grouse hunting that reflushing almost qualifies as a separate hunting sport. For one thing, a bird dog is not much help. In the small patchwork coverts where I do most of my hunting, flushed grouse more often than not alight in trees (usually conifers) well above the working range of a dog's nose.

You'd think that a grouse in a tree would be as obvious as a bowling ball on a billiard table, but it doesn't work that way. Grouse compress their feathers skintight to reduce body size when hiding on a branch, and then they hunker up against the tree trunk. Of course, sometimes they don't. And sometimes a once-flushed grouse will land on the ground and scurry for cover. My own experience, which may be more an apology for my various dogs over the years than a statement of solid fact, is that once-flushed grouse are far less tolerant of a dog's approach the second time around. The sport of reflushing is best performed – and most fully enjoyed – by the lone hunter.

The basic essential of reflushing is to watch where the grouse goes when first flushed. This isn't easy. We often get so caught up in the explosive drama of that initial encounter, what with the gasping and the shooting and then the missing, that visual tracking of the fleeing bird's path seems to be redundant to the main adventure.

Grouse have a knack for disappearing from sight once the trigger has been pulled. Actually, a grouse hunter can improve both his shooting and his hunting skills just by forming a habit of closely watching missed birds as they sail away beyond shotgun range. One way to do this is to always keep the gun aimed; don't bring it down so quickly in resignation and self-loathing.

A healthy grouse will seldom let you observe exactly where it lands. The challenge is to guess the location of that secret hideaway and develop a strategy for properly approaching it. The flight path will usually provide some clues, and it helps greatly if the covert is a familiar one. The first second or two of a flush is devoted more to speed and distance than to specific direction. It's the tail end of the final glide that reveals the bird's real objective. You can usually see a quick swerving to one side or the other as the grouse brakes for a landing and then darts into the foliage. Oftentimes this last maneuver is not visible to the hunter, in which case the final destination becomes doubly difficult to find.

Grouse generally seek two different types of landing sites. One is a definite hiding place deep in the shadows. The other is a short-range vantage point, some sort of a lookout from which the grouse can check you out and determine whether more distance should be added. To take the short-range type to an extreme, the first flush is sometimes no more than a quick jump into the nearest tree. Birds that take this route, and have not committed themselves to a full-blown escape, are not yet candidates for a well planned follow-up strategy. Instead, they are feathered bombs with short fuses, prepared to explode the instant you so much as take a step forward.

On the other hand, grouse that have hurtled all the way from ground zero to distant seclusion will often be reluctant to take to the air again until virtually forced to do so. These are the birds against which you must pit every ounce of your acquired skills. When a reflush does occur, it contains all the pent-up energy that a grouse can possibly store, for now such a bird will have no doubt about your intentions.

Finding a once-flushed grouse is only half the struggle, but it's the *first* half. Sometimes, right at the end of the initial flight, a clattering of wings will betray the distant refuge as the bird gropes for a more secure grip on its hastily found perch. When the flutter is heard, and when the direction of its final swerve in flight has been seen, the grouse can be reasonably pinpointed. If these clues are missing, follow-up becomes more a game of chance. I usually make a mental note of a specific landmark or tree close to where I think the grouse is lurking. This provides a focal point, a base around which a planned stalk can be made.

It's a good idea to avoid walking directly towards the suspected site. For one thing, a flushed grouse usually perches or comes to rest on the far side of a tree or blow-down. This means that the reflush will be unseen by the hunter who makes the mistake of a straightaway approach. Circling or coming in from a different angle places the grouse in a more vulnerable position when it finally takes to wing.

When following-up, I also try to guess in which direction the grouse will try to escape the second time, so I can "corner" the bird and perhaps be offered a better shot. Frankly, this doesn't work most of the time; but there are some situations in which I can predict with certainty that it will. One such situation occurs when a grouse has initially flown from the relatively open cover of dogwood or hawthorn bushes to the more dense edge of a conifer woods. You can bet that, on the next flush, the grouse will prefer to dive headlong into the depths of those woods. With this in mind, it only makes sense to approach the bird through the back door—from inside the woodline.

The hunter's mind has a subtle way of gathering a few scraps of almost intangible observation—the final tilt of the bird's fantail just before it disappears, a detected change in speed, perhaps the placement of certain conifers down the green alleyway which the winged plunge is taken—and then forging these scraps into a comfortable intuition that the grouse can only be . . . over *there*! When that magic spot is finally reached, the intuition is bolstered by an eerie feeling of being watched. If the guess has been a good one, the hunter *is* being watched—by a hidden grouse whose instincts are on full alert. This is a bird that will not flush unless the hunter moves in certain ways that signify intolerable threat. A once-flushed grouse, especially one that has just heard the gun, is inclined to wait until the hunter departs. Its genes are too familiar with the persistent ways of hawks that, having missed their prey on the first swoop, perch nearby, patiently awaiting a second chance at a bird in open flight.

The hunter can take his time, but the gun must be held ever ready. Now the grouse is less susceptible to stop-and-start or zigzag tactics. Proximity, sheer closeness, is what is needed to trigger the grouse into launching skyward again. Many steps may be taken with no results; then another trail, close by but covering merely the other sides of the same trees, is made. As it so often happens, the grouse finally erupts from a tree that was just a bit farther down the flight alleyway than your intuition had indicated.

The sound that Old Ruff's wings make when flushing from high in a tree is usually different from the familiar hollow thunder of a ground flush. There is less need to furiously churn the air in a climb for altitude. Instead, a grouse just dives off its perch and, with a few quick wingbeats, gains lightning speed. Obstructing branches are sometimes clattered against and left swaying. There is a commotion, to be sure, but the sound of flight is a mere echo of the original explosion from ground level.

The hunter has only part of an instant in which to react, usually less time than when the bird was first flushed. The cover in which reflushing is done is usually taller, if not thicker, and seldom is an open-sky, going-away shot offered. Oftentimes there will be no opportunity for shooting, and the hunter will have no recourse but to follow-up for yet another reflush.

When the ruffed grouse flushes from a tree, it often dives off its perch to gain speed before beating its wings. The sound this makes is different from a flush off the ground. *Photo by T. Martinson.*

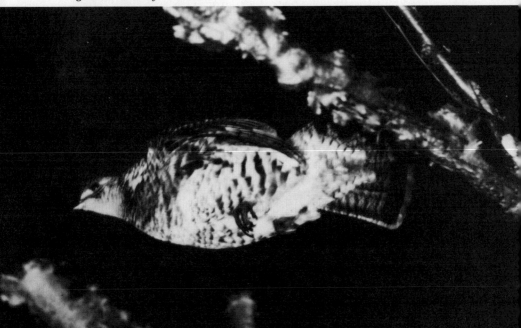

How to Ramble in the Brambles

The grouse hunter who goes into a covert without a dog has to work *like* a dog to get grouse moving. Sure, it's possible to flush an occasional grouse here and there by following logging roads and well-used deer trails. Eventually though, all the easy paths lead to a dead end, and a fellow who is serious about his sport knows that the only alternative is to plunge headlong into the brambles.

Those who attempt the first few yards and then enthusiastically wade on towards even greater challenges amid the pricker bushes are commonly called Grouse Hunters. The others—those who suddenly remember that the lawnmower needs to be repaired and then back away from the sharp teeth of that challenge, furtively sneaking back to civilization—become roadside groundhog hunters when the weather is nice and there's nothing good on television.

The outdoor world can be a scary place for indoor people. I firmly believe that the vast majority of anti-hunters have no concept of how much physical endeavor goes into the simple act of walking in the woods. Most of these people probably visualize the wild world in terms of lollipop trees and well-manicured lawns where game animals saunter (in the case of grouse) like chickens in a barnyard—the kind of scene a kindergartener might sketch. Even many birdwatchers and backpackers tend to view the wilderness in terms of what they've seen from well-marked trails or from boardwalks with glass-covered signs such as:

Cretaegus

–Over 550 species and varieties have been identified.
–Commonly called "hawthorn" or "thornapple."
–Warning: Thorns over 1 inch long.
DO NOT TOUCH!

By my way of thinking, an accurate comprehension of the outdoor world, of hunting, and of the niche that mankind holds in the realm of nature, can only be obtained by jumping right off the beaten path. This is certainly what experienced grouse hunters do, and they've got the scratches to prove it.

Maneuvering through the densely interlocked brambles of good grouse cover is not unlike swimming: you either make the right motions or you don't make any real progress. The covert-crawl is a different sort of stroke, but it gets you through the brush in good style.

In thick cover, a grouse hunter should always carry the gun in front of his face, pointed upward and outward for the possibility of a quick flush.

Wearing the right apparel, which includes brush chaps, a canvas or nylon jacket, hat, and shooting glasses, is necessary for keeping bodily harm to a minimum. But it's the right motions, plus a positive attitude and a good dose of patience, that keep the grouse hunter afloat in his favorite element.

I think I can claim that the most successful one-on-one grouse hunters are those who can do the deepest knee bends. A half-crouch is the position which most lone hunters are in when grouse flush in thick cover. Being able to spend hours walking and stalking in that position is, however, only one of the skills required for the covert-crawl. Something must be done to prevent low growth from constantly dragging against feet and legs.

I've settled over the years on a certain gait that seems to help. I call it the "peddle step." Instead of thrusting each foot directly forward as I would while walking on open ground, I take each step as though I were peddling a bicycle. This technique sounds goofy, but it works like a charm in thick goldenrod, berry briers, and other miscellaneous tangled ground cover. Each boot comes up from the ground *behind* the other leg until it's at knee level; then, and only then, I shove it forward to crunch downward on the pesky undergrowth. It really works. By also turning my lifted knee inward on each peddle step and placing one foot directly in front of the other, I part the weeds for easier passage.

When the going gets really tough, I shift down to whatever gear is necessary to maintain a comfortable pace. Not doing this is the mistake that leads to fatigue and irritation. I try not to think that a branch has purposely plucked off my hat; I remember instead that it was my head that hit the branch. After all, it's the ruffed grouse I'm after—not direct confrontation with the bird's habitat. A hawthorn is just a hawthorn, even if it does have sharp points and has obviously tried to attack me.

Sometimes a hunter can get so tied up in the intricacies of taking one more step, however awkwardly, that the gun becomes just so much cargo. That's a mistake. It's at moments like these—when the hunter holds the gun low or even behind him as he squirms through an opening—that grouse magically appear and then disappear. In thick cover, the gun's muzzle should always be out in front of the hunter's eyes, pointed both upward and outward. This position allows the gun barrel to protect the hunter's face from unkind branches and permits a faster mounting when a bird is flushed.

I have consciously formed a habit of literally following my gun through the tangles of grouse coverts. Where the gun can make passage, I too will probably fit. When I don't, we retreat and look for bigger gateways to ruffed grouse hideaways.

8

Hunting with Grouse Dogs

W hen you see a hunter walking into a grouse covert with a dog happily dashing on ahead, you somehow know that this fellow is not just another meat hunter. He's a sport hunter, a fellow who enjoys the companionship of a dog and the skilled teamwork involved in outwitting the canny grouse in the bird's own domain.

Casting a bird dog onward is much like springing a falcon loose from a leather-clad wrist. The spirit soars, temporarily freed from the two-footed shuffle of the human form. There is a certain symbiosis between hunter and bird dog, a mutually beneficial relationship which makes each a better performer in the uplands. The hunter provides transportation and guide service and he carries the gun, the claws and teeth of this predatory venture. The bird dog, nimble-footed and possessing a sense of smell keyed to the warm, feathery odors of wild grouse, locates game that it could not possibly capture alone.

For the hunter, the sight of a dog coursing through a covert, checking likely haunts and maneuvering to hunt hard without break-ing that slender thread of union between them, is a totally satisfying experience. Many hunters score a productive point or a proper flush as highly as a bird in the bag, whether they hit or miss. Some grouse hunters will not even shoot at a bird unless their dog has first made game; they count chance flushes as being no less opportunistic than pot shots or ground sluices.

You would think that the scenting and ground-covering abilities of a dog would provide tremendous advantages to the hunter. At first glance, it seems that all the hunter has to do is wait until his dog goes on point, and then wade into the cover to flush, shoot, and kill. Fortunately for the sport, matters aren't quite that simple. In fact, results of a hunter survey conducted several years ago by New York's Department of Environmental Conservation revealed that canine-ac-companied hunters annually bagged an average of only 20 percent more grouse than their dogless peers. That's not much of an advan-tage when compared with a 60 percent greater bag for pheasants, and 40 percent for rabbits.

Why this difference exists is fuel suitable for fireside debates. There are several possible arguments, all of which are valid to one degree or another. For one thing, the ruffed grouse is not an ordinary gamebird; consequently an ordinary bird dog is often no match at all for Bonasa. Sometimes, yes, but not often. A wily grouse seldom tolerates the clumsy approach of a half-trained or inexperienced dog, and it will be inclined to flush before the hunter can get into close position.

Said hunter will usually *see* more grouse in a year's time, but won't get to shoot at most of them. Even when forewarned by a properly pointed dog that a grouse lurks somewhere up ahead, the ordinary hunter approaches with no more confidence than if someone had tossed a sprung grenade into the bushes. Advance warning and the heightened anticipation that goes with it often serve only to in-crease tension—and tension leads to poor shooting.

Another likely reason why the average seasonal grouse take is so minimally influenced by dogs has something to do with the nature of the sport. Unlike pheasants and rabbits, ruffed grouse can be hunted without a dog *almost* as successfully as with a dog. It would seem that a hunter in partnership with a bird dog would find twice as many grouse, but this just isn't realistic. Usually, either the dog is hunting or the hunter is hunting. Dog-watching and -handling is a full-time job if done properly so that a dog's full potential can be realized in the upland coverts.

Some hunters may argue against this point, claiming instead that both they and their dogs are constantly hunting as partners. Perhaps, perhaps. In most instances, their dogs are short-ranged critters which seldom venture far enough from underfoot for it to be said that they are legitimately hunting on their own. In the opposite extreme, a fellow's dog may be so far-ranging that, in order to pass time until the dog is seen once again outlined against the horizon, the hunter goes ahead and hunts alone for grouse "with a dog along."

Then there are the dogs that really know their business. These rare creatures, grizzled veterans of the autumn brush wars, know that a ruffed grouse must be handled gingerly and at just the right and respectable distance. If such a dog's master is equally grizzled (at least in terms of experience), then close encounters with grouse will be more the rule than the exception. Unfortunately, seldom does such a gifted team have a chance to work together for more than a handful of years. One or the other of the partners will get stiff in the joints all too soon and have to forfeit the future to younger protagonists. But in the interim, what *treasure* they discover together!

The Ideal Grouse Dog

Somewhere between too close-ranging and too far-ranging is where the ideal grouse dog will be found. If said dog is a pointer and is truly ideal, it will be found, without much effort, staunchly on point. Or, if the dog is one of the breeds bred to flush first and ask questions later, then it will be close by and easily approached just prior to the crucial pounce.

Let's put aside for the moment the fact that most dogs are fun to be with, that sharing hunting experiences with household pets makes life richer, and that seeing our soul mirrored in a dog's moist eye is worthy of at least a sack of kibbles. Let's get a little cold-nosed ourselves. What is it, really, that a dog should rightfully be expected to do for us in strict terms of grouse hunting performance?

The answer is easy, once all the emotional paraphernalia is set aside temporarily. A grouse dog should be able to find more grouse than we would have found by ourselves, and then somehow communicate these finds to us—whether by the act of pointing or by a recognizable change in gait or posture—so we can move into effective shooting position. Short of having such expectations, the hunter is just a guy who likes dogs enough to tolerate the presence of one of them in a grouse covert.

Certain attributes are possessed by all ideal grouse dogs whether they are bred to point or to flush.

Responsiveness to Handling   There are many good grouse dogs that go unappreciated because, much of the time, they're hunting by themselves. The ideal grouse dog, on the other hand, hunts eagerly and brilliantly, but always for the hunter only. It hunts literally "for the gun" as surely and as loyally as a guide dog shoulders his blind master around an obstacle. The ideal grouse dog always knows where the hunter is and in which direction he's headed, and it will immediately react to commands from the master. Well . . . almost any command. The ideal dog will not make the mistake of breaking point if it *knows* a grouse is huddled nearby, not even if the hunter has whistled the go-ahead in disbelief that a bird is really there.

Scenting Skills   Any normal dog can smell a grouse, but it takes more than a good nose to make a good grouse dog. The ideal grouse dog takes most scent from the air currents, not from the ground. The ruffed grouse does not appreciate being trailed, and it will flush the instant it realizes that a snuffling dog is on its spoor. Regardless, a perpetual ground-sniffer would proceed much too slowly for upland hunting. The ideal dog adjusts both its speed and the direction from which it approaches a grouse haunt according to wind directions. Most importantly, the ideal dog reacts to grouse scent at the very instant of detection and does not risk a premature flush.

Birdiness   A truly birdy dog is interested even in the purring flights of passing sparrows. Such dogs begin whining when the end of summer brings cold winds, and they leap in ecstasy when leather boots are pulled from the closet. An ideal grouse dog, experienced and eager, will hunt with all the power of its heart every possible nook and cranny of a covert, undaunted by emptiness. If a bird is felled, such a dog will flatten foliage in attempts to find it. But once the dead bird has been brought to bag, the ideal grouse dog quests onward, to wherever the next grouse might be found.

Ground-Covering Effectiveness   Regardless of the breed, the ideal grouse dog always covers the area out in front of the hunter and never wastes time retracing steps. A proper dog casts back and forth across the hunter's field of view, ending each cast with a turn to the front rather than with a hook to the rear. But ground-covering should not be as mechanical as a windshield wiper. The ideal dog recognizes that grouse are most likely to be found lurking in certain types of cover, so he hunts accordingly, seeking grouse rather than sheer mileage or symmetry of pattern. The running pattern is adjusted to suit the habitat.

Range and Speed The opinions held among grouse hunters regarding ideal range and speed are as varied as their fingerprints. There really isn't an ideal range and speed; there are only special circumstances—and the ideal dog knows what they are. If the cover is very thick and visibility is poor, he will draw back and stay in closer to the hunter. Similarly, if scenting conditions are poor, the dog will shift down to a lower gear to avoid barging into grouse before their presence is detected by smell. But when the cover opens up and a light breeze quakes the aspen leaves, an ideal grouse dog will be hunting just inside the outer limits of his instincts.

This ability to adjust hunting style to the terrain and the hunter is a natural trait. Most bird dogs have it, but there are some who *always* hunt too close or too far from the gun. (Now we can get specific.) Sometimes, this behavior is the hunter's fault. Just as the ideal dog adjusts its style, so must the hunter adjust his own forward progress to accommodate the dog. Otherwise, a dog can get frustrated and quit hunting. Ironically, it is the ideal dog that is most sensitive to poor handling. This is because he is so responsive to the hunter's guidance, for better or for worse.

It's impossible to place a measurement on the perfect working range for a grouse dog. Certain pointing dogs of field trial bloodlines perform best for their masters while working a hundred yards or more out in front, coming back for a visual check-in every few minutes or so. It's only when the dog fails to reappear that the hunter begins looking for his dog—and the ideal dog will be found on point, not far from a grouse.

Other pointers, whether they be English pointers, English setters, or any of the Continental breeds, are sometimes genetically inclined to course a covert at decidedly shorter ranges. Most modern grouse hunters prefer to have their dogs remain in plain sight at least half of the time, or thereabouts. This preference is often based on distrust; hunters want to see their dogs start to make game so they can holler "Whoa!" and quickly smash through the briars to flush the bird themselves. The ideal dog does not require this sort of on-the-job training; he can be trusted to do his best without being supervised.

Flushing breeds, particularly the springer spaniel and Labrador retriever, can be ideal grouse dogs only if they are able to convey to their masters the message of a grouse discovery — while the bird is still on the ground. Via a stiffening of gait or furious tail-wagging, the dog notifies the hunter that a flush is imminent. Obviously, the ideal flushing dog works at considerably shorter range so the hunter can arrive on the scene before the headlong flushing plunge is made.

All ideal grouse dogs, whether they be pointers, flushers, or even mongrels that desire only to hunt grouse and care little for specific technique, share one attribute: They don't crowd the hunter. The first responsibility of an ideal dog is to locate grouse and warn the hunter *before* the hunter gets within flushing range. Otherwise, the hunter might as well be walking alone through the covert flushing grouse himself, unaided and unhampered by a bootlicking dog. A canine companion can be useful for finding fallen game, but that quality alone does not elevate a dog to ideal status.

Bold Confidence　A dog that can boldly crash through a covert will pin down more grouse for his master than a dog that slinks quietly and hesitates. The ruffed grouse is inclined to remain huddled in concealment if it believes danger will pass. To the grouse, the sight of a dog eagerly bouncing at high speed through a covert probably doesn't signify a direct threat. The bird waits, biding time. Then suddenly, there is silence. Danger seems imminent, yet is undefined. This stop-action pause in the "predatory pounce" freezes the bird with indecision.

The ideal pointer is a magician of sorts; in a single instant he can transform from an innocent passerby to the poised essence of threat. The ideal flushing dog often uses this trick too, although to a lesser extent. He pretends to not notice the bird until he makes a sudden sideways lunge. Equipped with bold confidence, regardless of breed, the ideal dog is not intimidated by the sharp thorns and gloomy shadows of a grouse covert. He plunges ever onward, never doubting, always seeking.

Favorite Grouse Dog Breeds

Until the last two decades or so, the English setter was the undisputed prince of classic ruffed grouse hunting. Even today, the art, literature, and fond reminiscences of grouse hunting portray the setter as the standard against which all other breeds must be measured. Certainly the long-legged gracefulness and wide-ranging speed of the dog influenced the manner in which the grouse was hunted.

In the earlier days of wood-paneled stationwagons, fewer sub-

The English setter: traditionally the classic grouse dog but losing ground in popularity.

urbs, and larger tracts of overgrown woodlands, a gentleman with his dog could hunt virtually anywhere he pleased. There was simply more space available in which a high-spirited dog could dash forth in carefree abandon. In the extreme, a fellow who attempted hunting with any other breed, with the possible exceptions of the English pointer, Irish setter, and Gordon setter, was considered a vulgar pretender.

Then things changed, gradually and with a complexity that an entire book would fall short of fully documenting. Rural lands were parceled into smaller acreages, the number of hunters increased, and several of the Continental breeds became popular in America. So did the springers and retrievers. All of these versatile breeds were shorter-ranged than the setter and possessed less classic style, but they handled more easily—and they proved to be effective grouse dogs. They seemed to better fit the needs for the majority of modern grouse hunters. There's potential for argument here. Whether the more recent arrivals deposed the English setter on the basis of grouse hunter preference or because they were, first and foremost, more suitable as household pets, is one very hot controversy.

As the following list shows, the English setter is still highly ranked in popularity among members of the Loyal Order of Dedicated Grouse Hunters. This ranking is based on the surveyed responses of 279 dog-owning grouse hunters following the 1981–1982 season. I'm not at all certain whether the results are statistically representative of *all* grouse dog-owners. It could well be that LODGH members are setting standards of their own. In any case, it seems reasonably obvious that the popularities of the Brittany spaniel (ranked first) and the German shorthair (ranked third) are indicative of a change in hunter

Some grouse hunters now are favoring closer-ranging and non-pointing breeds such as the Labrador retriever.

Grouse hunter preference in recent years for smaller, closer-ranging bird dogs has resulted in an increase in popularity for the Brittany spaniel.

preferences towards close-ranging dogs. Whether this is a change in the right direction is a matter of personal opinion. Ultimately, each hunter sets his own standards.

**Dog Breeds
Ranked in Order of
Popularity with Grouse Hunters**

Breed	*Hunter Preference %*
Brittany Spaniel	35.1
English Setter	31.5
German Shorthair	11.9
*Springer Spaniel	7.2
*Labrador Retriever	7.2
Gordon Setter	2.5
Irish Setter	1.0
*Golden Retriever	1.0
English Pointer	1.0
*Beagle	0.7
Weimaraner	0.4
Griffin	0.4
Mixed	0.4

*non-pointing breeds

Whistles and Bells: Sound Effects

When you're hunting for grouse with a dog *and* trying to pay attention to the direction you're headed *and* wading through tangled cover *and* attempting to keep an eye on the dog's progress, it's easy to lose concentration. And when concentration is lost, you next lose either your footing or the dog. Should a grouse flush then, you won't be ready for it.

If the dog is wearing a bell on its collar, however, the whole scenario of grouse hunting becomes more comfortable and relaxed. The gentle ringing of a dog's bell provides a lot of useful information, such as where the dog is and in which direction it's headed. If the sound of the bell stops, it can well mean that the dog is on point. (It can also mean, uh . . . something else oddly resembling a point.) By my way of thinking, a bell is so essential to the effectiveness of hunting with a bird dog that hunting without a bell is akin to driving at night without headlights.

Right behind a bell, I rank a dog whistle as the second most essential item for proper dog handling. I wear mine around my neck on a leather thong. One toot means "go ahead," two toots signify "come here." That's the whole repertoire. A dog's hearing is more responsive to high-pitched sounds and, anyway, whistling is easier than yelling.

Teaching a dog to respond to whistled rather than verbal commands is no problem at all. During the next few weekends afield use *both* types of command, one right after the other, and then switch totally to whistling. Whistling loudly enough to break icicles is not necessary; a soft note or two can be heard by bird dogs at remarkable distances.

That is, a whistle can be heard if the sound of the dog's bell doesn't interfere. Remember, a collar bell is only a few inches beneath the dog's ears. Cast metal bells that ring with near-constant vibrations are not suitable as dog bells, yet they are sold as such. I also don't care for the enclosed "acorn" horse harness bells (even though they shed sticky snow), because their constant tinkle is more appropriate for sleigh rides than grouse hunting.

My English pointer, Bridie, on point. When her brass bell stops ringing, I hold the gun ready. (*This* time, I held a camera.)

The best bird dog bells, in my opinion, are brass cow bells. They clunk once and then stop vibrating until the dog takes another step. The heavier the clapper, the better the bell, because it swings less often. There should be brief, silent periods in the ringing of a dog's bell so that the occasional whistled command can be clearly heard.

Ruffed grouse are surprisingly tolerant of all the commotion caused by bells and whistles. In fact, I have come to believe that a certain amount of ruckus and noise-making is an important element of this sport. Grouse seem less inclined to flush prematurely if they can determine the route of a dog's approach from the sound of the bell.

Look at it from the bird's point of view. A ruffed grouse simply cannot afford the caloric expenditure of a booming flush every time it hears a twig snap. Furthermore, in flight, the grouse becomes vulnerable to swooping attacks by hawks. Just being *seen* by a distant hawk can mean grave jeopardy for the reckless bird. The soul-chilling scream of an overhead hawk, by the way, sounds much like a hunter's whistle. I have a theory that says grouse sit tighter to the ground when they hear an extended blast of shrill whistling. Although I can't prove this, I'm convinced that whistling at least does not spook grouse into flushing. Consequently, when a dog I'm hunting with begins to stray too far or spend too much time sniffing a rabbit hole, I whistle as loudly and for as long as the situation warrants.

An experience that happened one crisp November afternoon many seasons ago first clued me into the possible benefits of whistling. I had become separated from my young English pointer (or rather, she had separated herself from me, as young dogs will do). After listening for some time, I finally heard the distant tinkle of Bridie's bell and headed off in its direction via a "shortcut" through a particularly dense thicket of thornapple trees. The thorns slowed me down, so I started whistling to the dog as I went. I didn't just toot a couple of times; I split the autumn air asunder with long shrill blasts. Finally, I paused in a small clearing, alternately whistling and calling until the dog found me in the thorny, tangled maze.

Bridie approached for the expected head-patting of reunion, but just before my hand touched her, she whirled sideways and froze on point. For a brief moment, I actually thought something was wrong with the dog. A grouse, hunkered down under the shadows of a bush not three yards distant from my boots, had refrained from flushing throughout all the noise and continued whistling. And it was a very healthy grouse! The bird erupted into a sky-shattering flush the instant I turned to peer into its lair. I shot and missed it—twice.

Even Brittanies, as well as all other capable dogs, should be leashed when the road-side is reached.

Other Essential Equipment

I like the company of a dog beside me on the front seat of a car. In fact, that's where my dogs ride when the next covert is only a mile or so down a rural road. Over a long haul, however, a dog should be confined to some sort of traveling crate or cage in the rear of the vehicle. Not only is this way best for a dog's protection at modern highway speeds, it's better for a dog's peace of mind. The little shelter of a dog crate provides a temporary respite from the high-strung drama of a day afield. An excited dog in the front seat always wants to help you drive; but in a crate, that same dog will curl up and take a relaxing snooze. I prefer the lightweight fiberglass crates used by airlines for shipping canine passengers. These can be purchased directly from the manufacturers, but I bought mine at the local commuter airport for a discounted price.

Another essential item for staying in control of a bird dog, when such control is needed, is a leash. I carry mine whenever I'm running a dog, regardless of where we happen to be. When we arrive back at the roadside far from where the car is parked, the leash goes on the dog. Or, as has happened a few times, a dog wearing a faceful of porcupine quills has been escorted on the leash directly from covert to the veterinarian's office. Under certain circumstances (usually unexpected), having a leash readily available can save you from more trouble than you ever thought a dog was capable of getting into.

Five Fundamentals of Pointer Training

Hunting with a truly good pointing grouse dog is one of those experiences which can be treasured for a lifetime. A dog that can properly handle grouse will literally lead you into a new dimension of grouse hunting, one in which the dog becomes an extension of your own psyche. New coverts will be discovered, and by relying on the instincts and scenting abilities of your canine partner, you will learn more about the daily haunts and habits of grouse.

If all birdhunters knew how really easy it can be to train a dog, the professional trainers would be forced out of business. Yet, if we were to assign dollar values to all the hours spent afield with the dog, if we tallied up all the added costs of pen-raised quail, dog food, dog housing, and other associated expenditures of do-it-yourself training, we would think twice before attempting to "save money." Here's how I look at it: Dog training is fun, it's recreation, and more is learned about what a given dog is capable of achieving.

The partnership of man and dog acquires even greater meaning for the grouse hunter who does his own training. There's something very special indeed about casting a home-trained dog forth into the woodlands; part of you goes with the dog, bounding off towards sweet mysteries.

The following five fundamental steps in training a pointer to work magic on grouse are merely the highlights of what is really required. There are many good books available on bird dog training, and I suggest that anyone interested in going the full distance alone should do as much reading on the subject as possible, before heading for the backyard with a dog in tow. (Actually, people don't tow bird dogs; bird dogs tow people.) You ultimately want a dog to be able to freeze a grouse into confused immobility by the act of sudden and decisive pointing—while still at a discreet, respectable distance from the bird. Caution and self-restraint are not natural traits, but a dog can learn them and thereby become a proper grouse dog.

1. The first, and perhaps most essential, step in a grouse dog training program is to teach your dog the "whoa" command. In a training situation or in the field, you want to be able to make the dog screech to a standing halt whenever you command "whoa!" Accomplishing this is far easier than you might think, even with a strong running dog; the command is most easily taught when the dog is still a pup—long before you introduce the dog to planted birds (pigeons, quail) and wild game.

At first, pose the pup in a normal standing position while softly repeating "whoa." Repetition and reward, again and again, will teach the dog the meaning of the word. When the dog will remain steady for a minute or so, it's time to teach "whoa" while the dog is being run on the end of a long leash or checkcord. It will be just like starting all over again; but with gentle tugs on the rope and judicious praise for good performance, you will soon have a dog that immediately stops all forward motion when you say the magic word. You may never be able to teach the dog to stay off the couch, but if the dog will "whoa," who cares?

The command "whoa" will come in handy in a variety of situations, and it serves importantly in grouse dog training as a basis of understanding and communication. The ruffed grouse is probably our most nervous gamebird. Other gamebirds, like the woodcock and bobwhite quail, will permit a hunting dog to approach very close before flushing. Not so the ruffed grouse; this grand gamebird requires delicate, special handling, and therefore the "whoa" command is likely to play a much more important role in training a grouse dog than it would with an "ordinary" bird dog. More about this later.

2. The second big step in training a grouse dog occurs when you introduce the dog to planted birds. Barn pigeons can be obtained relatively inexpensively. A pigeon can be dizzied for planting in the training field by tucking its head under a wing and rotating the whole bird several times. Domestic bobwhite quail don't need to be dizzied; they're cleaner and easier to keep, and they can be used over and over again if you keep several quail nearby in a call-back pen. This is a wire-mesh cage with a tapered 5-inch to 3-inch one-way funnel through which a loose quail can later be called by his caged mates. This call-back system works so successfully that as few as half a dozen quail can be more than enough for a bird dog's first year of training.

Why, you wonder, should there be a need for domestic birds in the training program of a grouse dog? The answer is that although many bird dogs are natural hunters and will perform adequately on pheasants and wild quail without having been taught the finer points of self-control, a true grouse dog must be taught early in his career to slam on the brakes the instant the scent of a hidden bird is detected. You can't teach a dog to do that unless you know in advance where a bird is hidden.

When planting a quail or pigeon, I usually kick a little tunnel into the overhanging grasses of the training field and place the bird in the tunnel head first. I also use gloves, and I follow a devious route to and from the plant site so as to not introduce my scent into the training exercise. When the dog is brought into the field (on a check-cord), it's wise to have the help of a second person to assist you.

Run the dog downwind from the planted bird, watching the dog carefully for those signs which indicate when the dog first detects the irresistible aroma of birdscent. When the dog's tail suddenly rides higher and the running gait stiffens into the beginnings of a prowl, you should command "whoa!" A young dog often will tug and jump against the restraining checkcord, so work your way up the rope to the dog and physically settle him into a standing position. Praise the dog; let him know what a grand beast he is for having found a bird!

Pass the rope to your willing assistant, and walk in from the side to flush the bird. Delay this if the dog starts acting up again. You want the dog to be pointing (or at least standing still) when you finally do flush the bird. At the flush, discharge a starter's pistol or shotgun into the air. On occasion you may want to kill a bird for the dog, but this practice can be carried too far—and it's expensive. Ultimately, the dog will learn that it is fun to just find and *hold* birds by pointing, so that you can do the flushing. In other words, you don't need to purpose-fully develop a bloodlust in a grouse dog. Obviously, the "whoa" command is an essential step in communicating to the dog what his piece of the action is supposed to be.

3. Step three involves an adjustment of the young dog's ground-running pattern. Although many dogs will naturally run—and stay—out in front of you, this desirable trait can be further enhanced with proper training. You also want the dog to learn to keep checking on your location so that, later in the grouse woods, the dog won't pick up the bad habit of expecting you to find him. That can be tough.

During exercise periods and off-season romps in the woods, walk a zigzag route so that the young dog must keep an eye on you or else be left behind. Each time you change direction, softly call "hey!" or some other one-syllable expression. The running dog will learn to automatically turn in the direction of that sound—but without coming all the way back in to you. Some dogs tend to hook towards your backtrail, which can be a very annoying and unproductive trait. This can be dealt with by surprising and startling the dog when the rear-ward hook first begins. Shout loudly and begin running in the oppo-site direction, away from the dog. Clap your hands, whistle, or what-ever. But by no means should you permit the dog to dawdle in the rear.

These romps in the field are also good times to get extra practice on "whoa." At first, you may be able to enforce "whoa" only while the dog is within petting distance. Later, you should be able to call out the command over a hundred yards or more and see your dog turn into a motionless statue. When this happens, always walk to the dog and praise him first, before sending him on ahead. This type of friendly contact and firm control will serve you well on those occasions when a fledgling grouse dog first begins to run wild, drunk on the scent of lurking grouse.

4. The most difficult part of training a grouse dog is right here in step four—and it's something that *you*, not the dog, have to learn. Let's say that it is now October. The dog has learned to "whoa," will happily point planted domestic birds without flushing them, and dashes over a front running ground pattern regardless of which way you venture through the grouse coverts. You have high expectations; the dog appears fully trained. But just as that thought clears, you hear the thudding sound of a grouse exploding into flight. Right in gun range!

Hold on there just a minute. Don't shoot. Don't reward the dog for having bumped that grouse! Just an accident, you say, the dog couldn't help it. Maybe, maybe, I say, but the dog must not be allowed to get into the habit of flushing grouse. That's *your* job.

You should not harshly discipline the dog for a mistake that might not have been intentional. Instead, "whoa" the dog. You might even consider picking the dog up and carrying him farther downwind from the flush site. Put him on "whoa" again. Then, return to where the grouse took its departure, and pretend to search for the bird, using the same deliberate actions that you have earlier used with the dog on planted birds. Obviously failing to locate the grouse, go back to the dog. Praise the dog for remaining in place. Your next move (and this is important) is to grasp the dog's collar and steer him away from this place. Neither of you will gain anything by messing around in the vicinity of stale grouse scent and failed expectations.

5. This is where the whole thing falls into place, with every part fitting snugly and staying that way. Step five is the graduate course in grouse hunting. You need to make a commitment, both for yourself and the dog, to keep backsliding to an absolute minimum. A few months of training do not result in a permanently trained dog. There is a natural tendency on the part of the amateur handler to succumb to mediocrity. The dog begins to make mistakes which the hunter over-looks as being unimportant, forgivable and forgettable. After all, if a

fellow can accept certain faults in his human friends, then why not do the same for the family dog, right?

The fallacy here is not in the intent, but in a lack of understanding of animal behavior. A dog, unless otherwise educated, has no sense of right and wrong. If a dog is permitted without reprimand to crowd a grouse too closely, then it *learns* to crowd grouse. It's plain and simple: If you let a dog do something, you're *teaching* the dog to do it. (Why, for example, do many bird dog-owners let their pets break point, and yet swat the critters when they chew on the furniture? Talk about a double standard!)

The high-strung nature of the ruffed grouse demands that a grouse dog meet certain standards of excellence. Other species of gamebirds (especially woodcock) can make a mediocre bird dog look like a champion, but unless the amateur maintains a proper continuing education for his dog, season after season, both he and the dog will eventually fail together in their chosen sport.

How to Approach a Dog on Point

When a dog finally detects grouse scent and freezes on point, the dog's job is finished. Now it becomes the hunter's responsibility to move to the front and flush the bird from wherever it might be concealed. The dog should be kept on point throughout this venture, or else it will soon backslide and start to flush solely for the pleasure of hearing grouse thunder. (Okay, *sometimes* a truly exceptional pointer can be taught to perform both functions for other gamebirds, but seldom for grouse, at least not year after year.)

As soon as the hunter realizes that his dog is on point, he should walk briskly towards the area. There is a tendency to want to sneak up quietly, but grouse seem to hold more tightly during a quick, noisy approach. This doesn't always work, but the hunter can usually help himself by shortening the shooting range in as brief a time as possible. I always try to circle around past the dog and come in from the side. This way, I can watch the dog for clues as to where the bird might be lurking *and* I can view the probable launch site before plunging in for the flush. Besides, barging right past a faithfully pointing dog has always struck me as being rash, if not impolite. Once I'm within what seems to be reasonable shotgun range, I pause for a moment to assess the situation. I also, out of the corner of my mouth, tell the dog what a grand beast he or she is for having brought me this far. "Good dog. Now . . . *whoa*, dammit!"

Not knowing exactly where the bird is hidden is a considerable handicap. When the grouse does finally flush, it will almost certainly select the moment when you are in the worst possible shooting position, and it does this on purpose. The best strategy under such circumstances is to use available clues as to where the bird most likely will be found and where it will try to fly.

First, be aware that grouse seldom fly back over the pointed dog. If it weren't for the intimidating presence of said dog, the bird probably would have left when the hunter first arrived. When it isn't immediately obvious to me that the grouse is in such-and-such a location, I look to the dog for guidance. If the point has lost some of its slobbering intensity, I conclude that the grouse has either flushed before I arrived, or that it has walked far enough away that the dog is no longer smelling fresh birdscent. But, if the dog is still alertly peering into the shadows, unmoving except for an occasional quiver, I give close scrutiny to what lies before me.

The next clue is the direction of the wind. Having hunted with a variety of pointing dogs, I find that the direction indicated by a dog's head and body is not necessarily the way to a hidden bird. More often, it seems, a grouse will be found upwind from the dog, regardless of the dog's posture. I look for openings in the overhead foliage, passageways where a grouse can escape. Next I try to imagine which

Always approach a pointing dog from the side, not from the rear. This will improve chances for a better shot, and the dog is less apt to break point.

way a grouse would prefer to flush. After these few seconds of pondering both my situation and that of my prey, I step forward, committed to specific action whether right or wrong. I kick the underbrush, stop and start, zig and zag, and do everything that rightfully ought to result in thunder. If these actions don't work, I look to the dog to see whether I'm doing things correctly. Oftentimes an experienced dog will shift posture slightly when the hunter has failed to produce a find. This time, believe the dog and follow the direction that is now indicated. "Oh . . . over *there!*"

When it is finally driven from concealment, the grouse will thrill the dog as much as it thrills you. If the dog is young and inexperienced, or old but stale from boredom, shoot the gun whether or not an honest shot is offered. The dog will appreciate your involvement in the specialness of having found and flushed a ruffed grouse.

How to Know When You're Not Having Fun

Not every bird dog is intended by genetic design and fate to become an authentic grouse dog. Many otherwise good dogs just don't make the grade; they try but fail under the demands presented by a gamebird that has the personality of nitroglycerin. A dog that constantly bumps into grouse knows only the sights and sounds of wasteful explosions. A grouse hunter should invest one year, perhaps even two or three years, in a young dog before any judgment of the future is made. (Most bird dogs don't reach their full potential until they're at least four years old.) Ultimately, however, a decision needs to be reached: either the dog has what it takes to be a grouse dog, or it doesn't. Too often, grouse hunters squander a decade or more of life's short seasons in the uplands with dogs that would rather chase rabbits or deer than hunt grouse.

Of course, if it's just companionship you're really wanting from a dog, then that's a different matter. One of the most enjoyable dogs I ever hunted with was a beagle-dachshund mongrel. Krista had absolutely no style and even less class, but she possessed unbounded enthusiasm for finding grouse. Looking back, I doubt that she ever produced grouse that I wouldn't have flushed anyway. My favorite mongrel wasn't a real grouse dog by any stretch of the imagination, but hunting with her was always a joy, however innocent.

During the intervening years I've gone the whole route with bird dog field trialing, and have done my own training also for upland bird hunting. I've won a few ribbons and even a trophy or two for these efforts. But where I've really gained during the years of experience has been in my awareness of how remarkably a properly trained bird dog can perform. Unfortunately, many hunters more easily believe the claimed feats of sheep dogs, St. Bernards, and guide dogs for the blind; it just doesn't seem possible to them that a bird dog can be trusted to perform equally well at its own special endeavor. When a dog owner settles for less, he usually gets even less than he expected. Even the sole redeeming virtue of companionship loses some of its flavor when spoiled by constantly poor performance.

Too often, a hunter will continue to tolerate year after year the annoyances and hindrances of an unworthy dog, to the point that the allure of grouse hunting has fizzled entirely. I say, get rid of such dogs. If spouse and offspring grope at your hunting chaps and beg that Old Bootlicker be spared from a listing under DOGS FOR SALE, then let *them* feed and care for the sorry animal. But don't take that dog into the grouse coverts again. Know when to quit. If the thought of hunting with the family pet sort of puts a knot in your stomach, making advertisements for louder whistles and electronic shock collars look appealing, then go hunting alone—or buy another puppy and start over again.

9

Winter Grouse Hunting

When winter arrives, the sport of grouse hunting enters a different dimension. Gone are the splendors of autumn, swept away by cold winds. You can forget about foraging for ripe wild apples for a noonday snack. No longer is it a pleasant experience to rest upon one of those picturesque (now achingly frigid) stone walls. Gone too are most of the traditional aspects of grouse hunting techniques.

Winter alters the outlands to the extent that even our favorite coverts appear to be inhospitable territory to hunter and hunted alike. But don't let appearances fool you; the ruffed grouse is a very adaptive, hardy gamebird. Like its cousin the Arctic ptarmigan, it can survive and even thrive in the rigors of a frozen world. If you can make an honest attempt to adjust your hunting technique to the changed habitat and behaviors of grouse in winter, you will discover a truly different sport.

Grouse hunting in winter offers many side benefits, some tangible, others not so easily measured. The forest in winter acquires a dimension of rare beauty not easily detected from the salt-spattered highways. The hunter pays his only dues by the effort of hoofing it back off the road. At first, the landscape appears bleak, a black-and-white montage of stark, bare limbs against the dead gleam of fallen snow. The eye soon adapts and becomes sensitive to subtle colors and reflections. Just when you are totally distracted by the beauty of a winter world, summer-like thunder erupts. Oops! There goes a grouse, flying hell-bent for cover. Your gloved fingers grope clumsily for the gun's safety and trigger. You swing, shoot, and, well, probably miss. That's one thing about grouse hunting that doesn't change with the seasons: those birds are *always* hard to hit!

Nevertheless, winter grouse hunting carries with it certain measures of predictability that the autumn season lacks. For one thing, winter grouse can be found more easily, and in less time afield. This is because the altered habitat provides not necessarily *less* food and shelter, but a lesser *variety* of both. If you know where to look, the odds are good that grouse will be found there. We'll talk about that later. Another aspect of winter hunting that favors the hunter is the absence of leaves on the trees, which provides better visibility for shots at longer ranges. And with the onset of colder weather, there usually are fewer hunters afield.

The only real disadvantage of winter hunting is that the whole scenario is a bit less comfortable if you're not prepared for the cold weather. But if you're willing to abide the lack of autumnal pleasures (such as eating wild apples and all that stuff), and replace them instead with the simple joys of physical endeavor, you will discover that winter grouse hunting is a sport that distills the principle of fair chase to its purest form. You are the hunter, and ruffed grouse is the hunted. Tracks left in the snow will testify to who won, in terms of hit or miss. But in terms of opportunities given, the winter grouse hunter is always the winner.

The Late Season

Late season grouse hunting is not just the tail end of something better, like that long part of a T-bone steak which usually doesn't get eaten. Sure, the winter side of this sport of ours has always played second fiddle to the earlier season in grouse hunting literature. The glories of autumn present a hard act to follow. But let's not carry this bit about the mystique of the autumn woodlands too far. The fall of the year is mostly a pleasant time, but it is also a period of change—changes that take place almost on a weekly basis. I often don't even bother to hunt during the first week or two of the opening season in western New York State (where I live), simply because the weather can be so hot and uncomfortable, the foliage so thick and impenetrable, that such a venture would be more work than pleasure.

With the passage of October into November, autumn opens another door, one that leads to real treasures of ripeness and fulfillment. It is of this truly magical period that most good grouse stories have been written. Unfortunately, hallowed autumn lasts for only three or four weeks. Something happens that shatters the magic: it's called "deer season."

Whether or not you join the crowd (I do too, but I am weak), the woodlands change in the interim. A few weeks later, when the hue and cry have ended, we are faced with—winter. Is this the end of our outdoor sporting adventures? Well, for many upland game hunters, it is. For some reason that I have not yet fathomed (and I've truly tried), the majority of hunters of all kinds stalk other game—namely televised sports.

There is a minority of hunters, dedicated souls one and all, who have discovered the real pleasures and advantages of winter grouse hunting. Fewer hunters afield, for example, means simply that we're less likely to cross one another's path. Grouse hunters are not unsociable, but it's always with heartfelt joy that we find our favorite coverts empty of other hunters. Solitude has no real value if you can't depend on its durability.

The terrain of winter woodlands is more agreeable, too. You find fewer burrs that cling and fewer thorns that rake, no mosquitoes and other obnoxious bugs, and nary a snake, poisonous or otherwise. Nor will you encounter poison ivy, heat stroke, flies, and that bane of all hard-hunting grousers, the sweaty itch.

Properly outfitted, the winter hunter enjoys a more comfortable environment while the stay-at-home sportsfolk miss out on good hunting. Ha! I'd rather hunt in a screaming blizzard than during a hot, muggy day—and I've done it both ways, many, many times. In fact, I probably log as many grouse hunting hours during the winter as in the autumn. (Yes, a quick check of my written record for last year confirms it.) Admittedly, there are more sunlit hours in October and early November, which permit longer stretches of hunting time and more frequent-but-brief hunts in late afternoon after the chores are done. ("Uh, thanks Honey, but I'll eat when I get back"; that sort of thing.)

The ruffed grouse is a very adaptive and hardy gamebird, able to survive and even thrive during the meanest weather winter can bring. Fluffed-out feathers provide extra warmth, making bird appear "plump as a partridge." *Photo by T. Martinson.*

The waning winter sun cuts late-afternoon opportunities short. However, in most states where grouse are hunted—and there are at least 27 of 'em—the grouse season extends well into the next year. In my home state of New York, the grouse season is open from the first day of October to the very last day of February. That's five solid months, nearly half a year, and the *majority* of that period is smack-dab in the dead of winter. Around here, when cars won't start, we figure that the grouse season is still open. Over the long haul, the late season totals up more potential hunting hours just because it stays around longer and creates more weekends than holy autumn ever could.

Many other states have extended their grouse seasons, particularly during the last ten years, so that dedicated wingshots (like you and me, right?) can more fully participate in the recreation of winter hunting. You begin to wonder *which* end of this bounty is the tail and which is the tenderloin—autumn or winter. Some brushworn grouse hunters, having stumbled tired and torn from the autumn coverts only to discover that their state conservation department has extended the season, respond with such comments as, "Enough is enough!" They move on to adventures presumably more satisfying, such as putting a new floor in the bathroom. Other veterans of the brush wars, instinctively recognizing opportunity when they see it, turn on their heels and re-enter the woods as though ordered to do so. Considered by some to be cruel and unusual punishment, the extended months of grouse season are, to the stalwart, prizes worthy of endeavor—like mountains, they are there.

There are those among us who believe that grouse seasons should have early closing dates. Their logic is based on the belief that overhunting (that's the word they use) will result in the destruction of breeding stock for next year's crop. They are partly right. Too much hunting pressure in an isolated covert can temporarily teeter the natural balance and totter the prospect of good grouse hunting for the next year. Generally, however, the random autumn dispersal of young grouse from adjacent coverts will re-seed an overgunned covert.

An excess of hunting pressure in every covert over a long period of time could, of course, destroy grouse hunting as we now know it. But the fewer grouse there are to hunt, the fewer hunters there will be willing to try to hunt them. Heck, you couldn't *pay* folks to go out in the dead of winter to seek the last remnants of a grouse population. The ruffed grouse is an evasive bird under the best of circumstances, difficult to find and even more difficult to center in a pattern of birdshot.

It matters little to the ruffed grouse population whether the season is a month or a year, or whether the daily bag limit is two, four, or even a hundred grouse. The hunter who bags a single grouse is as happy then as a puppy with a bone—and maybe even a little happier. He knows intuitively that a long time may pass before another grouse falls to the ground. Wildlife biologists and game managers, whose job it is to permit as much recreational activity as a natural resource can provide without being damaged, believe that the extended grouse season is a good idea. I agree with them.

A hunter can learn a great deal about grouse habits by following their tracks in the snow. Distance between prints is usually only about an inch; longer strides mean the bird is running.

Here's a listing of all the states that hold open season on grouse, grouped according to the month in which their 1982 seasons closed. These dates might be changed, of course, as time goes by, but it's a good bet that those changes will lead to even longer seasons.

Ruffed Grouse Season Closing Dates		
November	*December*	*March*
Maine	Michigan	Alaska
	Minnesota	
	New Hampshire	
	Vermont	
January	*February*	
Connecticut	Georgia	
Iowa	Kentucky	
Indiana	New Jersey	
Maryland	New York	
Massachusetts	North Carolina	
Pennsylvania	Ohio	
South Carolina	Rhode Island	
Virginia	Tennessee	
Wisconsin	West Virginia	

(California, Washington, and North Dakota have earlier closing dates than those shown above. There also are presently at least two other states whose wildlife agencies are involved in programs to introduce the ruffed grouse.)

How and Where to Hunt Winter Grouse

How you hunt winter grouse depends on where you find 'em. This is not a totally off-the-wall statement. Time of day and weather conditions have considerable influence on where grouse can be found within the range of a covert. This in turn affects your hunting techniques.

During the autumn, you can meander through Ruff's domain at random, without specific objectives in mind, and still be fairly certain of putting up a bird here and there. In the winter, you might follow this same route day after day and never see so much as a single grouse. Whether you are on the magic path or several yards off-course can mean the difference between having nearby grouse flush at your approach, or merely sit tight and watch you slog on by. The margin for this kind of tactical error needs to be reckoned with during the winter season.

Winter habitat becomes more sharply defined by the carving away of autumn's bounty, with fewer options open to grouse for shelter and food supply. New foods appear, chiefly the awakening buds of poplar, wild cherry, and birch trees, but the *variety* of available foods is definitely diminished. Add to this the fact that there simply are fewer grouse left from the spring broods, and your chances of running into a bird that's not where it's ecologically supposed to be are mighty slim.

Grouse generally remain in the coverts where they settled following the "fall shuffle," the random dispersal of young flocks. What this means to the winter hunter is that coverts which contained grouse in November will likely host many of these same birds later in winter. Sure, a winter covert can appear barren of grouse, if you hunt it wrong and without a plan. But if you hit the sweet spot, you'll unlock the thunder of wings, often many times over.

There's something almost magic about the way the ruffed grouse eludes even our best efforts. The only trait you can rely on is his unpredictability. Still, if a magic act is repeated often enough and watched by enough observers, a pattern begins to emerge.

Such a pattern was discerned in New York State, when research was being done in preparation for that classic book, *The Ruffed Grouse*, by Bump, Darrow, Edminster, and Crissey, published back in 1947. Studies on 5,347 recorded grouse flushes revealed that grouse become less terrestrial when winter arrives. That is, they spend more time aloft in trees. The following table illustrates this tendency.

	Seasonal Preference of Grouse for Trees or Ground (% of Flushes)	
	Autumn	*Winter*
Trees	10.8	37.8
Ground	89.2	62.2

At first glance, this bit of information might not seem particularly important. But let me give you some of my interpretations of the numbers. First, they tell me that grouse are 3½ times more likely to flush out of a tree in the winter as in the autumn. To put it another way, grouse in winter are only two-thirds as likely to be found under the same ground cover where you jumped 'em last autumn. If nothing else, these comparisons tell you that your success in winter hunting will be more than a little under par if you don't alter hunting tactics accordingly.

The word *trees* in terms of grouse roosting almost always means conifers: the pines, spruce, hemlocks, and other evergreens whose dense structures provide shelter from the wind, seclusion from soaring hawks, and right-sized branches for perching. I'd sooner pass up an entire forest of bare-branched deciduous trees than a tight little clump of pines nestled at the woodside, if I want to flush a grouse. The odds are roughly two to one (according to the research data) that the grouse will be on the ground. But I guarantee, the birds won't be more than the distance of one quick, short flush away from that inviting clump of pines, if there are grouse anywhere to be found.

You hunt grouse by hunting habitat. That's a plain and simple formula for proper participation in the sport. If the grouse hunter sounds more like a botanist than a hunter, it's because he knows his game and its habitat better than the run-of-the-mill gunner. Other hunters can stumble around the woods and maybe put out a rabbit or see a squirrel. Or they sit on a stump somewhere and hope that a deer comes by. The grouse hunter is stuck with the premise that nothing but *Bonasa umbellus* in the bag will constitute a prize for effort.

You flush grouse by placing yourself so close to them that, in a sudden roar of flight, they reveal their presence. Even against the blank white backdrop of winter, you will seldom actually see a grouse until it has spread wings and churned the air into a vortex of spinning air. To seek a view of lurking grouse is usually a waste of time. By itself, the discovery of a winter covert, containing all the ecologically balanced elements of good habitat and even revealing the existence of grouse by the telltale signs of their tracks in the snow, is still no guarantee that you'll get any shooting opportunities.

You must first physically pass through that magic, ever-changing threshold into the realm where a grouse instantly and instinctively figures there's not room enough for the both of you. The bird flushes; *then* you've "found" a grouse. Sometimes that threshold is thirty yards away from the epicenter of a grouse explosion. At other times it's more like three yards. You never know when the invisible lever has been tripped until there's a sudden roaring of wings.

In winter, the grouse hunter must hunt more purposefully, entering intimately into the habitat until he literally can't see the forest for the trees. In the autumn, grouse can be found just about anywhere in

Grouse in winter are confined to a smaller range in their coverts, and don't spend as much time on the ground as they do during autumn. *Photo by T. Martinson.*

a covert—sometimes even where they shouldn't be—and a hunter can stumble onto stray birds as though he knew what he was doing. The winter grouse hunter, on the other hand, needs a full tank of hustle-and-know-how (sometimes known as "luck") to get into the thick of the action.

Down the hill from where I live, across the road and on the other side of a small hayfield, there's an irregularly shaped covert that encompasses probably forty acres in the autumn. But in winter, when the hawthorns, brushy viburnum, and berry tangles are neither fruitful nor affording of shelter from the wind, the covert shrinks down to a fragmented total of about ten acres of conifers.

I know this covert and its feathered occupants very well, because I use it as a dog-training area. This ten-acre range, which doesn't sound like much if you're thinking in terms of one hole on a golf course or the parking lot of a small shopping mall, is plenty enough territory to fill an entire winter afternoon with grouse hunting. In fact, there's about a three-acre edging of hemlock and wild cherry at the far end, overlooking a gently sloping pasture, that's worth at least half an hour's hard hunting. I took three winter grouse from that one little patch just before writing this chapter and left at least four others there (and I think there were more) before closing the book on the season.

I've logged many hours and trekked many miles through those few close-to-home acres, but never have I been able to predict exactly where a grouse could be found. Sometimes it even appeared to me that grouse had entirely deserted the area. The point here is that although I know this small covert like the back of my hand, my knowledge has revealed no secret shortcuts which might have bypassed the sporting ethic. I still have to work hard for every grouse I manage to flush, and even harder for every grouse that offers a decent chance at a shot. What I've learned in a quarter century of ruffed grouse hunting is that the quality of a covert, particularly in winter, cannot be measured by the results of one or two brief forays.

When you are provided the opportunity to hunt a new winter covert, first time ever, try to find where the grouse are according to the weather and time of day, and use some sort of plan. I've outlined various strategies in the following chart.

Although grouse seldom travel more than a few hundred yards within the ecological confines of their winter coverts, they are very responsive to any change in conditions and will relocate as is necessary to keep in harmony with the natural order of things. If you're also in tune with the effects of those changes, you will find grouse — provided you work at it.

The Frost Phoenix and the Buckbrush Secret

Ruffed grouse often display a winter trait that betrays some of their other tricks for eluding hunters. Although it seems hardly possible that a gamebird would bury itself in deep snow to hide from the elements and predators alike, that is exactly what grouse do if conditions are right. *Snow-roosting* has been well documented by game biologists, and any hunter who ventures into the deep, fresh snow of a winter covert in the northern states will likely make a similar observation.

The discovery of a snow-roosted grouse is always a surprise. You just don't expect the snow to erupt in a wild explosion of winged thunder. The experience can definitely make you swallow your gum. But if you're planning to hunt winter grouse, you had better consider looking for snow-roosted grouse as part of the game plan.

There are mixed opinions as to how grouse manage to get under the snow in the first place. The traditional belief is that they plunge headlong into the snow, like comets falling out of the sky. Obviously if

Checklist for the Winter Grouse Hunter

Time of Day	Weather Conditions	Best Way to Hunt
Early morning and late afternoon	Cold, high winds and deep, fluffy snow	Seek snow-roosted grouse. Look for tracks leading to snow tunnels, and investigate any unexplained disturbance in the snow. Search edges of coverts near open hardwoods and fencerows where snow has drifted.
Early morning and late afternoon	Snow crusted or only 1–2 inches deep. Mild temperatures, light breeze or still air.	Search small clumps of evergreens near stands of poplar, wild cherry, or birch trees. Be aware that grouse are likely to be on the snow. Look for tracks if snow permits.
Midday hours	Cold, high winds; any type of snow cover or bare frozen ground.	Cautiously probe the edges of thick evergreens, such as plantation pine. Walk slowly, especially on the downside from the wind. Also check out bushy ravines and other sheltered areas. In the latter areas, look to the ground for grouse.
Midday hours	Balmy blue skies, no wind, and soggy, wet snow with thawed patches or no snow at all.	Think as an autumn hunter does. Seek thick brushy cover close to berry briars, hawthorns, spring seeps, thawed patches, and small, isolated islands of evergreens.
Any time of day	Overcast or indifferent skies, no wind. Good tracking snow left over from previous evening.	Put a real effort into finding tracks in the snow—then follow them. If trail ends with marks of wingtips in snow, look ahead in nearest evergreens for roosting grouse.

the snow isn't sufficiently deep to cushion the impact, grouse can be injured in such dramatic exploits. But there is considerable evidence that grouse do, in fact, take the plunge – particularly when being pursued by a hawk. A different school of thought holds that grouse first land gently on the surface of the snow and then wriggle and shuffle themselves down under cover.

Both techniques have been reported by wildlife biologists, and I myself have read the telltale signs in the snow that substantiate both theories. Most often, however, my observations afield have been that grouse stroll through the woodlands for considerable distances before burrowing headfirst into the snow. Even with this evidence of tracks and obvious entry, you can never be sure just where a grouse is lurking, because snow-roosting grouse often tunnel under the snow for distances of a dozen feet or more. Sometimes it's only a yard or less.

If drifting snow has swept away all signs of entry, the stage is set for an even greater surprise when Old Ruff explodes out of his frozen lair. This sudden unlocking of the earth, of scattered ice crystals forming in midair into a feathered fury of living motion, is the stuff of which myths are made. For the hunter, this experience is enough to instill belief in the legend of the phoenix, that mysterious bird which rose from ashes of fire to live again. You don't get to see such miracles by staying home on a cold day when you could be hunting!

Grouse do most of their snow-roosting from dusk to dawn, sheltering themselves from winter winds and predators during the sunless hours. However, a sharp drop in temperature or a stiff wind will drive grouse into the white stuff at any time of day. There is evidence (based on the size of the pile of droppings that grouse invariably leave behind in their snow roosts) that grouse sometimes remain underground for two or three days at a stretch. I have stumbled upon snow-roosting grouse many times when the sun was already high in the sky.

Grouse lurk there beneath the surface protected also by a keen sense of hearing; the lightest of threatening footfalls can trigger a rapid escape. According to Dr. Gordon Gullion, emminent ruffed grouse researcher at the University of Minnesota, the only raptor which poses any real danger to snow-roosted grouse is the great grey owl of the northern coniferous forests. Another researcher, Steve Loch, has reasoned that these large night birds are able to hear grouse in their snow roosts. The lynx, prowling on out-sized padded feet, also is known to be adept at taking grouse from under the snow.

My own close encounters show that a hunter, too, can approach

To the winter grouse hunter, this is a beautiful sight: the droppings left by a snow-roosted grouse. If fresh, the bird is probably nearby.

within virtual grabbing distance of a snow-roosting grouse. There have been many times when I could have swatted grouse out of the air with a tennis racket or caught them in a fishing net, had I been so equipped and so inclined to do such silly things.

A major goal I set for myself during the winter I began writing this book was to capture a grouse on film, as it exploded into flight. My obsession was to take a photograph that would dramatically portray the icy violence of a winter flush, complete with snow spraying every which way and with the grouse's wings spread wide, stabbing at the air for even greater speed. All I ever got was snow on my face and pictures of blurs that only I knew were grouse. I felt that my dedication, my temporary willingness to leave the gun at home, would be rewarded somehow by the high-speed photo of a lifetime spent outdoors.

But that didn't happen. My only reward was that I learned how to approach a snow-roosted grouse close enough to make a close-up photo physically possible. I discovered that, by lowering my feet very slowly into the snow on each step and by not letting my shadow cross the grouse's suspected lair, I was able to shove the camera lens to within a yard of the grouse when it first appeared. Unfortunately, my reactions were never quite fast enough at that range to release the shutter in time.

One day I put five grouse into the air out of one small snowdrift. If I'd been toting a shotgun, I might have scored both a double and a triple in the space of a few seconds. (This, of course, would have been a difficult feat with the double-barreled shotgun I usually carry! Two shots are all I get, period.)

Another thing I learned about grouse is that they rarely snow-roost in the same area from one day to the next. I had expected my close scrutiny to reveal that the grouse followed a pattern, but instead they were unpredictable. I discovered an area where several grouse had once roosted in the middle of an open pasture, at least a hundred yards from the nearest trees! Eventually I gave up on my photography project and returned to the role of hunter. I gained from the experience, and I will be a better winter grouse hunter because of it.

That's the whole point of this dissertation on snow-roosting. We tend to expect ruffed grouse to behave like ordinary birds simply because they have feathers. On the contrary, grouse act more like rabbits and other land-based creatures. To successfully hunt grouse, we need to think of grouse as the gallinaceous, ground-scratching, terrestrial gamebirds that they are. It just will not suffice to hunt looking *up*, when grouse are most likely underfoot. This basic truth brings us to the "buckbrush secret," something I've never read about elsewhere, but have discovered time and time again while hunting winter grouse in snow-covered habitat.

Simply stated, the buckbrush secret amounts to one fact: winter grouse often lurk under the bowed stalks of berry bushes, dogwood, viburnum, and any other kind of growth that bends over when laden with snow. Yeah sure, you say, grouse hide under bushes in autumn too, so what's the big deal? The important difference is that winter

Look under the snow-bowed branches of dogwood, viburnum, and other bushes for ruffed grouse. Sometimes grouse even stay overnight in these snug shelters when snow is too crusted for normal snow-roosting.

grouse don't just hide under these bushes; they *stay* there. Relatively large snow caves are formed under the overhanging branches of buckbrush, and the protection from bitter weather and flying predators is much the same as with snow-roosting, except that there's a lot more space for moving about and maybe even pecking at a dried berry or two.

Snow-roosting is virtually impossible for grouse when the snow has crusted over as the result of warming temperatures. It's my observation that grouse choose the buckbrush maneuver as a viable alternative under these circumstances. (Not all the time, of course; you could go hungry betting on what a grouse will do.) Whenever I find a grouse under the buckbrush, I usually flush two or three more birds during the ensuing minutes of floundering around in this always-heavy cover. Don't ask me how a group of grouse are able to agree on a common course of behavior. Just be aware that, in winter, the ruffed grouse is a more social bird. Perhaps it's because the harsh conditions of an altered habitat narrow the options for the ruffed grouse.

I know of several buckbrush areas within the two dozen or so coverts that I annually haunt, and it's to these select spots that I go first during the winter. I kick the snow-covered brush, clamber through it, and poke and probe for possible thunder. You've got to be really close to buckbrush grouse to get them moving. If this turns out to be futile exercise, I switch my attention to possible snow-roosting sites where the snow is soft and fluffy. Then I seek small clearings and the forest's edge where blowing winds have drifted the snow to greater depths. Finally, if I have not yet found where the grouse are congregated, I head for the pines, the hemlocks, the spruce—the coniferous cover where the cold bite of winter is partially muzzled.

Hunting the Evergreens in Winter

Hunting the snow-laden evergreens for grouse is a unique aspect of our sport which, in terms of sheer thrill and excitement, is surpassed only by the once-in-a-lifetime experience of tracking a Cape buffalo or wounded lion into the long grass. Ruffed grouse routinely use the element of surprise at any time of the season to avoid being in the center of a shot pattern, and they're good at it. But back in the shadows of dense stands of pine, spruce, or hemlock, where grouse lurk during the midday hours of winter, their explosive off-your-shoulder flushes are more apt to strike terror than mere surprise in the hearts of their pursuers.

The habitat I'm describing often takes the form of small pine plantations that are between ten and twenty years old—thick, but not impenetrable. Wherever you find poplar and wild cherry trees banked alongside such conifer stands in the outlands, grouse action is a distinct possibility. Similar habitat often borders more mature forest and lowland marshes.

Grouse are loath to depart this type of balanced cover and they usually fly only short distances from it—most often to another conifer from which they can keep an eye on your progress. Once flushed and newly concealed, Ruff is twice as hard to flush again. You have to stalk carefully and very slowly. Walk too fast and the hidden bird will let you pass right on by.

If you goof up your second chance at a shot, you can darn near get within arm's length of a grouse before he will take off again. Even at this close range, Old Ruff has a fantastic ability to remain hidden. He will fold his feathers tight against the skin, making himself as thin as a hungry weasel. Then he will creep right down next to the trunk of the tree, usually opposite the side of your initial approach. In order to flush, he has to shuffle outward along the limb to get take-off room.

Often, just as the grouse spreads his wings, he will utter a soft alarm, "cuk-cuk," and then blast off in a cloud of powdered snow. But most of the time the grouse will stay put. One way to get him to move a little and reveal his position is for you to stand absolutely still, listening intently. The grouse may get nervous and move along the perch to get a better look at you. (A bird dog is virtually useless on treed grouse, except to locate fallen game.)

When a grouse finally explodes into a branch-busting flush, your inclination will be to whip off a snap shot, especially if the bird scared you silly by knocking snow right down the back of your neck. Don't take that first shot at close range. Try to track the bird's flight and take him at an opening in the trees. If you don't get that opportunity, listen for the sound of the grouse as he plunges through pine branches to a new roost. (That's something you can rarely do in autumn.) Deep winter grouse don't travel far, so hold your fire if you can't get an honest shot. You'll probably get another chance.

This kind of hunting can really tax your ability as a wingshot. This is where a season's percentage can drop many points in a single afternoon. You often get two separate glimpses of the bird in flight—first at ultra-close range, then an instant later at thirty or forty yards when the grouse momentarily clears the tops of the conifers. The choice of choke and shot size under these conditions should be based on *which* of these two extremes best suits your individual shooting style. Believe it or not, there's a lot to be said for taking the longer shot with a tight choke and coarse shot, even No. 4s. This combination is particularly effective when a heavy snowfall has decorated the evergreens with a layer of insulating snow.

Snow is a real shot-stopper, especially if the white stuff has been exposed for a couple of hours to sunlight and rising temperatures. Light shot just doesn't get through a packing snow. Even soft powder snow will bust your pattern wide open. And on days when the evergreens are snow-covered, the "see-thru" ability is poor. At long ranges, the skeet bore gunner is handicapped.

When two hunters work parallel along the edge of plantation pine, however, the shooting distances can be shortened. One man does the work, shoving his way through the trees about ten or fifteen yards in from the edge. The other hunter lags quietly behind, out in the open. Grouse perched in these fringe trees will invariably pop out in the open in front of the second man. At least half of the time, a tricky grouse will try to fly behind the hunter that flushed him, thereby providing a crossing overhead shot to the gunner in the open. In this situation, an open bored shotgun is no drawback.

If you find one grouse in the conifers, there's almost always another one lurking nearby. I've never had a chance at a double, though, back in the evergreens. The birds flush one at a time, and you never know when you've finally got the last one airborne. Don't relax for a second. The only way to take a breather is to get the heck out in the open. It gives you a chance to pick the snow out of your ears.

No one in his right mind would knock the traditional pleasures of those first Indian summer weeks of grouse season. There's nothing else quite like it. And I enjoy the company of a good bird dog as much as the next guy. But for my money, no other technique of grouse hunting comes close to providing the excitement of stalking a wary grouse, a grouse that has flushed once and will do so again at any second, with a roar of chestnut-brown wings beating up through white-frosted branches.

When to Leave the Dog at Home

Grouse can be successfully hunted without the help of a dog at any time during the season. Many hunters have scored big on grouse for years on end without ever having seen a bird dog go on point. When you hunt for grouse, you're actually hunting for grouse *habitat*; you don't need to sniff the wind to identify poplars or grapevines or evergreens. In winter, grouse habitat is even more sharply defined. The colder the weather and the deeper the snow, the less you need a dog to help locate grouse. Sure, grouse will see you coming, but their instinct is to remain concealed until you have approached within a distance that conveniently (for us) falls inside shotgun range. Grouse flush not because you have found them; no, they explode into flight when you step inside the range of their built-in, biological proximity fuses. *Then* you see grouse!

Grouse in wintertime are more experienced, more mature, than the birds of autumn. The majority were hatched during the previous spring, and are the survivors of almost daily threats by hawks, owls, foxes, and hunters. The dumb and slow have been selectively removed from the population, and those grouse that remain are cagey critters with much less tolerance for the close approach of a dog. Grouse also seem to be aware that their natural camouflage is less effective against a backdrop of white snow.

My point is that a bird dog contributes little to the success of a winter hunt and can even mess up a good day by bumping grouse outside gun range. (My No. 1 dog would bite me if she could read this.)

Hear me out, bird dog lovers. In true winter habitat, which in the northern reaches of grouse country means drifted snow, cold wind, and relatively poor scenting conditions, a dog will reap more frustration than feathers. A dog just can't perform under such conditions. You couldn't either, with frost on your muzzle and a cold tail. Let a January thaw come along, though, and I'll jump at the opportunity to cast my dog off to the uplands. The balmy, bare-bones days following a thaw are better even than October for hunting grouse with a dog. When winter comes howling back, stripping away the warmth and locking the outlands in a crystalline embrace, I leave the bird dog home. The only kind of dog I'd consider taking then would be the sort that sleeps under the snow, eats raw fish, and runs faster when you holler "Mush!"

Some Tips for Cold-Weather Comfort

I've leaned into a cold wind often enough to know what pain is, but I'm going to take some shortcuts here and leave out all that stuff about how to dress warmly. This is a grouse hunter's guide, not a manual for Arctic explorers.

Ironically, the winter hunter's main problem is not in protecting himself from the cold, but in preventing overheating and *then* getting chilled. You bull your way through tangles of pricker bushes, sometimes crunch through deep snow, and generally get a generous supply of exercise while seeking Old Ruff. Building up a sweat is easy; preventing one isn't. Nevertheless, just a few extra accommodations to the bitter elements can mean the difference between a good hunt and one from which you return feeling more like a survivor than a hunter. You want to be a threat to the grouse, not to yourself.

A hooded sweatshirt, one that zips up the front, is a downright handy piece of apparel for the winter hunter. I wear mine over a sweater, and over them both I usually add a long-sleeved canvas hunting coat that has a gamebag. The hood of the sweatshirt slips snugly over my head when I need temporary protection from the wind, and it comes off quickly and conveniently when so desired. The advantage of having a hood means that I can wear a less warm hat, just something to keep the snow out of my hair. When I feel myself starting to overheat, I can unzip both the game jacket and sweatshirt to provide some welcome ventilation. If mere unzipping doesn't do the job, I remove either the sweater or the sweatshirt and place it in my gamebag.

Sometimes, however, only a temporary cool-off is needed. You may have, for example, just climbed a steep hill and the exertion has put you on the verge of a sweat. The terrain ahead appears to be easygoing—not warranting a permanent stripdown. When this situation occurs, try the following maneuver for fast air-conditioning: Remove your outer garments (the jacket and sweatshirt), wave them around in the cool air and then, just before the cold begins to penetrate your skin, put everything right back on. Your excess body heat can now be absorbed by the cooled clothing, and you will have maintained a neat balance between too-hot and too-cold.

Gloves are probably the greatest hindrance to the winter grouse hunter. It's amazing how that extra half second required to poke a gloved finger around the trigger can mean the difference between hit or miss. Of course, if your hands are too cold, you can't get off a good shot anyway. The cold steel of a shotgun, tightly gripped for long periods of time, acts like a sponge to soak up whatever precious bit of heat remains in your extremities. I've solved only half this problem. I occasionally wear a thicker glove on my left hand, and a thin cotton workglove on my right hand. The combination looks sort of goofy, sure, but the thin glove lets me slip the shooting hand into a warm pocket when numbness strikes.

Polarized sunglasses not only filter the glare of sunlit snow, they also serve to divert the cold wind away from your eyes. You should always be wearing some sort of shooting glasses anyway, to protect your sight from whipping branches and other jagged dangers. In colder weather, glasses with plastic rims are decidedly more comfortable than those with metal rims.

If you have ever been plagued by snow filling into your boot tops, try leaving your pants untucked so that the cuffs hang loosely around the ankles. It's amazing how well this works, even in very deep snow. You may also be pleasantly surprised by what a set of old-fashioned suspenders can do to reduce the fatigue in your legs and lower back. When you have to wade through thick brush and snow drifts, a lot of high stepping is required. A belt tends to ride low towards the end of a long day, causing the pants-legs to bind the flexing of your knees. Suspenders, on the other hand, help you at every stride with a gentle lifting motion. I've found that wearing suspenders sometimes results in a little stiffness in the shoulders, but my legs always come through a journey afield just like new from the factory.

Finally, if you have any thoughts of ever sitting down for a rest on a snowy day, I suggest you keep a plastic bag handy. Your backside may be dragging, but you can still keep it warm and dry.

10

The Grouse Hunter's Log

There has been so much emphasis on *tradition* in the literature of grouse hunting, and often so much value placed on *style* during fireside debate, that it must seem to the novice that the grouse season is open to club members only. If ever there was a hunting sport left wide open for accusations of elitism, it is ruffed grouse hunting. At least, on the face of it.

At times, grouse hunters do seem to stand apart from hunters of other game. For example, seldom do you encounter other hunters who are as reluctant to discuss exactly where they hunt and what their body-count "score" is. Or who are quite as slow to extend an invitation to hunt with them next weekend. Yes, it could be said that the typical grouse hunter behaves a tad strangely. But there are solid reasons for this. Frankly, it really isn't easy to act normal *and* be a dedicated grouse hunter.

For one thing, too much grouse thunder can drive you crazy. But so can too little. It's the constant hair-trigger expectancy that keeps us ever alert and even a little twitchy. Experts say they have no evidence that grouse can fly faster than fifty miles per hour, and I believe them. That is, I believe that they have no evidence. Any real grouse hunter already knows that Old Ruff can beat Mach One in the first second of flight. That explosion you hear is obviously a sonic boom. I've had grouse bust out from underfoot with such fantastic speed that I didn't even *see* them go! This is proof that grouse can sometimes fly even faster than the speed of light.

We retreat emotionally, in the face of these blurred challenges to our shooting skills, and we construct little protective shelters for our egos. The grouse hunter's solemn homage to ritual and style, and his heightened appreciation of autumn in all its splendid forms, are symptoms of something greater than just a desire to kill birds. We want to be able to look down, see our boots on the ground and feel reassured that it was dedication and not dementia that brought us into a covert. So, we substitute ritual for habit, apply style in place of indifferent technique, and feel better for having done so.

Another Quirk: The Logbook

We also maintain logs of our grouse hunting activities. It's perhaps just another ritual, but the act of writing down the events of a day afield can be an enriching addition to the sport. If nothing else, the written words later provide us with a tangible record of our participation in a sport which contains many seemingly intangible aspects. The discovery of a new covert, a remarkable performance of dogwork, a thrilling opportunity for a grouse double that fell apart at the last second—these are no less real than the final tally of the kill. The logbook itself can be anything from a dog-eared card stored in the glove compartment of a pickup truck to a leatherbound volume that reposes on a handsome book shelf. It doesn't matter which, or where in between. One fellow I know maintains a log by inking entries of birds flushed/shot-at/killed/and date/ on a steel column in the factory where he works.

While the cold hard facts of hit-and-miss are perhaps the most basic measure of grouse hunting experience, they nevertheless provide a frame of reference for reminiscence. Add the *where* and the *how* and you've got all the elements needed for a full-blown reconstruction of what really happened, many years down the pike. I daresay that with the help of my grouse hunter's log, I could recall and then relive at least the better parts of any day I've ever spent in a grouse covert.

The ruffed grouse: the cause of our dementia that we call "dedication."

But a logbook can be a storehouse for a lot more than just fuel for generating memories. It can be a useful tool for helping a grouse hunter to find better ways and places to hunt.

Grouse hunting puts special demands on its followers in ways that are different from virtually all other hunting sports. For one thing, coverts are never quite the same from one year to the next. Grouse habitat is a fragile ecosystem that exists in pockets at the woodline between meadows and mature forests. This "edge" cover is forever advancing towards a sterile maturity that only fire or the machines of man can forestall.

Most coverts provide optimum conditions for ruffed grouse for only a few years. Then the hardwood trees shade the poplar and birch into oblivion; the evergreen trees stretch too tall and spread their branches too widely for grouse to find snug shelter; and the bushes and brambles dwindle and disappear. These changes may seem ponderously slow—yet they aren't. Subtle shifts in the ecological balance of a covert can be observed annually, but only if you're looking for them.

The grouse, however, is far more responsive to any shift in the balance of its habitat. The grouse population will decline at a far greater rate than that of the obvious, visual changes in a covert. Still, a hunter will continue to visit coverts well past their prime year after year, enticed more by recollections of good times past than by the reality of the present. If a fellow is in the habit of making certain routine entries in a logbook, however, his evaluation of a covert will be well-grounded in fact. It's all right to fool other hunters—but not oneself.

For all practical purposes, the best measure of the viability of a grouse covert is the average ratio of *flushes-per-hour*. It's the individual hunter who determines whether all grouse seen and heard are to be counted and recorded, or just those birds which flush within shotgun range. If the ratio is to be interpreted as an indication of grouse population, then every bird (except obvious reflushes) should be included in the tally. Many hunters, however, apply flushes-per-hour as a yardstick against which to gauge their own ability to approach grouse, and consequently count a flush only if it occurs within a reasonable distance from the gun. There's obviously much overlap here, since each and every hunter's concept of what's "close" or "far" is somewhat different.

But over the long haul, the number of flushes counted, divided by the total hours spent in a covert, provides a hunter with a valuable clue to the worth of a grouse covert. If his logbook shows a steady decline in flushes-per-hour over a few years' time for a specific covert, yet other coverts continue to hold their own or even improve, it may be more than appropriate to cross this place off autumn's itinerary.

It can really hurt when a favorite covert passes through the threshold of forest maturity and no longer contains grouse in huntable numbers. I can recall many such former coverts, some that I still occasionally drive past just to say hello. There's one special place where I buried a good dog; she got old and passed on at just about the time the covert took the same trip. They had both been young and eager for grouse when we first hunted there. It wasn't until I'd lost the covert *and* the dog in the same year that I realized how short-lived a covert can be.

Apparently no one else knew that grouse were abundant there. I always had the place to myself and, in a way, I still do. I'm certain that the only existing record that here was once one of the sweetest coverts ever shared by man and dog is in the pages of my logbook.

I don't think that I'd ever purposely show this log to anyone. For one thing, my past records of shooting successes are generally down-right laughable. Hit-and-miss should be a personal matter anyway, just like the balance of the old checkbook and certain other things that other folks don't really need to know about. Perhaps the keeper of any grouse hunting log should stash his personal records in a hollow log or keep a hole dug in the back lawn for emergencies (such as THE END).

Personally, I try not to be a score-keeper, at least when it comes to grouse hunting. But I do want to know on a year-to-year basis whether any improvement in my shooting skills has occurred. There's certainly room for it. I record *flushes/shots/and hits* as faithfully as though I were paid to do so.

I even evaluate my dogs, not because they need to justify their food bill, but because I want to be able to remember with accuracy when it's my turn to be proud.

October 23, 1983, near Big Tree: Found Bridie on point by the beaver pond. When I got beside her, a grouse flushed to left. Missed it. Then another grouse went straightaway. Missed again. While reloading, another grouse went up. Closed gun, stepped ahead and a 4th grouse took off. Missed. Dog's point softened then and so I walked back to release her from point. Flushed a woodcock along the way. Got it!

During those sixty seconds my grouse "hits 'n' misses" ratio took a left turn and veered wildly off the road. But Bridie's stock soared. She scored a "5" for *productive points* in that one encounter, and it's all right there in my log.

Pointing dogs will occasionally, for some unknown reason, go on point and yet not produce a grouse. Or a dog may barge in so close to a grouse that the bird flushes as soon as the dog halts. Neither of these circumstances is truly a productive point. The record should reflect an honest image of what's really happening out there in grouse country. It's only when the hunter is able to flush a grouse that the dog has first located, that a true find should be credited.

Aside from being a chronicle of past exploits (the flushing and the shooting and the dog things), a grouse hunter's logbook is a prime source of *places to hunt*. It's human nature for us to believe that we can remember all the good coverts without the help of lists and the writ-ten word. Maybe we can, given enough time for reflection. But au-tumn is brief, a quick passage of golden days.

My own concept of a fulfilled grouse hunting season is measured not in bag tallies, but in how many really good coverts I can visit in the short time alloted. And I have found that memory is inadequate when there are but a couple of hours of sunlight left and I'm trying to get my vehicle in gear while the dog is whining in anticipation of birdscent. Fortunately, I carry a long list of grouse covert names in my wallet. It's a condensed version of a detailed section in my logbook, where I store valuable bits of information such as roadside observations of distant poplar hillsides and fragments of conversations overheard at Ruffed Grouse Society banquets—and any other clues that might provide me with the whereabouts of yet another covert.

Many of the coverts on my list have become annual favorites; others I've hunted only a few times. Some coverts I haven't even *seen* yet; they're identified as "possibles" and in certain ways these mystery coverts are even more enticing than my familiar haunts. It is a genuine thrill when the discovery of a new covert is made. There is a feeling of personal renewal, a vague realization that the boundaries of life can be pushed outward when we really need the extra space.

Naked Truth About the "Typical" Grouse Hunter

The hard, cold statistic of *grouse killed per year* is the one logbook entry which conveys a meaning distinct from all the other entries. The number of birds brought to bag seems more a measure of shooting than hunting skills. Yet, if you get right down to it, the final body count is the bottom line on the total ledger of points, flushes, shots fired, and hours spent afield. There are few (if any) dedicated grouse hunters who need to check a scoresheet to determine whether their time spent afield was enjoyable. But I've never met a grouse hunter who couldn't rattle off his annual kills for at least the last few seasons. There is apparently something very important here, some clue to the specialness of ruffed grouse hunting.

A major appeal of this sport is that it is difficult to be good at. Knowing this, each of us strives to be at least better-than-average (whatever that means) in order to have some assurance that we are "doing-it-right." And for this we need a measure, a means of comparison with fellow hunters. We're not talking competitiveness here, but the setting of common standards. With deer hunting this is easy. "Gitcher deer?" is answered with either a yes or a no. Small-game hunters usually shoot a "mess" or even a "limit" of squirrels, rabbits, doves or ducks every time they go afield. But the grouse hunter, more often than not, comes home empty-handed. Listeners tire quickly of tales of missed shots. If they're grouse hunters, they already know the feeling. If they're not, how can they understand the thrill of *almost* getting something?

We generally disdain scorekeeping as being irrelevant to full enjoyment of the sport. Yet we eagerly turn to any available grouse-kill data in much the same way we check out the centerfold of certain magazines before reading the articles. The naked truth about grouse hunting can be seen in the following chart of "Hunter Success Rates." Data for this chart was provided by Ken Szabo, publisher of *Grouse Tales*, and it's based on the results logged by 350 of the members of the Loyal Order of Dedicated Grouse Hunters at the end of the 1982-83 season.

It's important for you to understand that this chart represents shooting successes of real grouse hunters, *not* the sum total for all hunters who just happened to buy a small-game license. Dedicated grouse hunters tend to be purists; the sport itself demands a certain commitment and doesn't leave much time for mixed-bag hunting. Consider also that the respondents in this survey were sufficiently devoted to grouse hunting to maintain logs of their upland activities. I make this point for the sake of the legitimacy of the data. If you feel a need to compare your annual kill results with authentic grouse hunters from across the nation, this is the place to do it.

The chart is a simple graph of the numbers of grouse killed per year versus the percent of survey respondents who managed to kill those various numbers of birds. Right away, you can see that the highest percentages of hunters killed only a few birds.

How do *you* compare? Find the number (on the horizontal line) of the grouse you bagged last year. Straight above it is the percent of dedicated grouse hunters who killed the same numbers of birds. Now, add up all the percents to the left of your position on the chart. The sum will be the total percent of hunters who got fewer grouse than you did. Now that you know the Truth, does it really matter?

Let's look at the data from some other viewpoints not shown on the chart.

1. The *average* number of grouse killed per hunter is 10.3 birds. But average in this case is not "typical," as I will explain.
2. The *median* number of grouse felled is a somewhat more accurate way to define the middle ground of grouse hunting's successes. That is, half the hunters dropped fewer than 5.3 grouse. The other half got more than that.
3. The *mode* is the most common number of grouse killed, the number that represents the largest group of hunters. The mode is the value that people generally interpret as being "typical." But look at

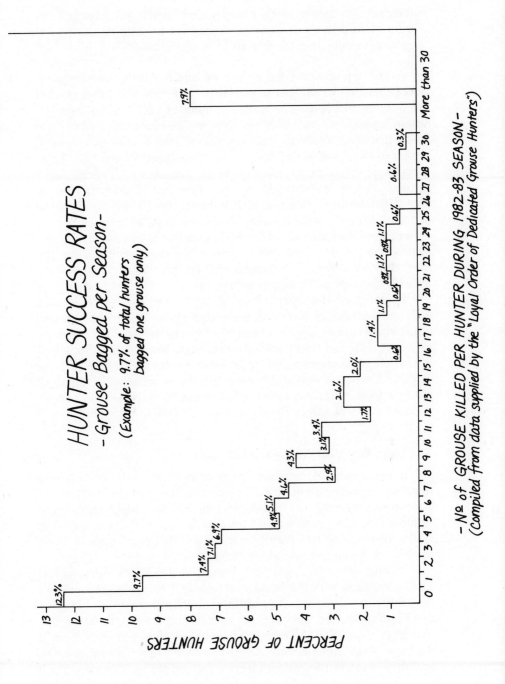

HUNTER SUCCESS RATES
-Grouse Bagged per Season-
(Example: 9.7% of total hunters bagged one grouse only)

PERCENT OF GROUSE HUNTERS

12.3% 9.7% 7.4% 7.1% 6.9% 5.1% 4.9% 4.9% 4.6% 4.3% 3.4% 3.1% 2.9% 2.6% 2.0% 1.7% 1.4% 1.1% 1.1% 0.9% 1.1% 0.9% 0.6% 0.6% 0.6% 0.3% 0.6% 7.9%

- N⁰ of GROUSE KILLED PER HUNTER DURING 1982-83 SEASON -
(Compiled from data supplied by the "Loyal Order of Dedicated Grouse Hunters")

the chart: the largest single group of dedicated hunters bagged *zero* grouse! And that's as close as we can get to defining the typical grouse hunter using the fine art of statistical analysis.

At the opposite end of the chart we find the intriguing statistic of "more than 30" grouse-per-season that were killed by 7.9 percent of the hunters surveyed. The actual number of birds in this category ranges from 31 to a high of 74 per hunter. The sum total of all of them is 34.6 percent of *all* the grouse bagged in the whole survey! What this means to the sport is definitely a matter of personal opinion. Reactions I've observed range from admiration and envy on through disbelief and cries of "game hog!" My own view rests peacefully close to respect for the dedication these fellow hunters must have for the sport of grouse hunting. Whereas these few souls could have opted to hunt easier game and *really* score high body-counts, they pitted themselves against the thunder bird and walked many, many miles along the more difficult pathway. One could say that this trait of dogged determination is "typical" of all grouse hunters.

In reality, off the charted page, the typical grouse hunter is more truly represented by each and every one of the 350 grouse hunters who helped us make these statistical comparisons. (I should say these *silly* comparisons.) Every one of these hunters enters the domain of the ruffed grouse from a slightly different direction, carrying different skills and expectations, and hoping that his or her special choice of gun/gauge/shot size/dog breed/style of hunting/and covert is the combination that will unlock the treasure of personal achievement.

The Little Trophies: Photos and Fantails

In every sense of the word, an ink-heavy logbook is one of grouse hunting's finest trophies. It's all there: the hits and the misses, the adventures, the dogs, the friends, and the coverts. Most ruffed grouse hunters who have been around for a while wouldn't trade their logbooks for anything less than a fresh, new listing of a hundred secret coverts, with time granted to use 'em all.

Photographs are a rich contribution to a hunter's memory file. They gain value with the passage of time and help to keep a fellow's remembrances in focus. (Young hunters snap pictures of dogs and dead birds. Later on, they include friends and coverts, realizing that change is a way of life.) The best time to carry a camera afield is *all* of the time. Many cameras today weigh less than a handful of shotshells, and they're worth the bother. Just one picture of Pup's first point will

A grouse fantail being pinned into full spread. Each feather must be held or gaps will appear during drying. Insert each pin at an angle alongside quill so that feather will be held against backboard.

justify the inconvenience of an extra hard lump in the gamebag for an entire season.

Collecting grouse fantails is yet another way that a hunter can maintain a visible record of past successes. Each fantail is slightly different in color and markings, and a display of fantails, on a den wall or under the glass of a coffee table, can bring back in a single glance all the memories of halcyon days afield. The fantail spreads to a full 180 degrees and will remain in that position if the feathers are smoothed and pinned into place during a couple weeks of drying. (Table salt or laundry borax applied at the base of the tail will preserve such trophies for decades.)

Logbooks, photos, and fantails don't, of course, improve your hunting skills. Ruffed grouse will fall or flee regardless of any intent on your part to document the outcome of encounters with them. Instead, it's the value you place in yourself as a sportsman that will be reflected in the pages and the little trophies of your grouse hunting adventures.

11

From Covert to Kitchen

In ruffed grouse hunting, the focus of attention seems always to be on either the challenge or the splendor. Certainly just the sport itself, even considering the thorn scratches and the missed shots, is sufficient reward to keep a fellow's boots trudging ever onward. Grouse are grandly evasive birds, and therein lies the thrill of hunting them. But every once in a while someone actually *kills* one.

It does happen that way sometimes, not as often as we prefer, but with just enough frequency to whet our appetite for more. The ruffed grouse definitely qualifies as a rare fowl of gourmet status. Even if only the difficulty of acquiring and the true cost of our efforts were to be considered, we could rank grouse flesh with peacock tongue as being an exclusive delicacy.

To the ancient Romans, the partridge was a symbol of ribaldry; they also prized its flesh as an aphrodisiac. I can make no such claims for present-day North American ruffed grouse (except that eating them makes me love hunting them all the more). I will contend, however, that a meal of ruffed grouse, if proper precautions have been taken both in the covert and the kitchen, is an unforgetable experience.

Consider the uniqueness of grouse flesh. The breast is white meat, and the legs are dark. With many gamebirds it's just the opposite. The wild duck, goose, dove, rail, snipe, and woodcock are migratory birds that have been engineered by nature for long, sustained flights. Consequently, their breast muscles are engorged with blood vessels and capillaries, which make the flesh appear dark. Even the sharptail grouse, close cousin of the ruffed grouse, is dark-breasted to accommodate its long flights across the endless prairies. Only the pheasant, quail, and wild turkey, along with the ruffed grouse, provide ample bites of tender white meat.

There is yet another difference, one that sets the ruffed grouse apart from all other gamebirds. This is the virtual absence of fat in its meat. Because its winter diet can consist chiefly of tree buds (which sprout in winter as well as in spring), grouse need to store less fat than any other gamebird. This absence of fat requires that the chef take special precautions during the cooking of ruffed grouse. But they're worth it. The tart berries, buds, and other wild foods which the ruffed grouse feasts upon impart a special flavor that the discerning palate can truly appreciate.

The contents of a grouse's crop can provide some very useful clues for the grouse hunter. If you can determine which wild foods the bird has recently eaten, then the odds are good that other grouse will be found in or near the same type of habitat where such foods grow. Remember, the availability of berries and buds is ever-changing with the forward shift of the seasons. What grouse are feeding upon one week might be passé the next.

A thin membrane under the base of the bird's neck, the crop is external to the body, yet under the feathered skin. It can easily be opened for examination by probing a thumb forcefully between the crop and the bird's neck. The whole berries and buds, bits of leaves, apples or whatever, will be fresh and sweet-smelling. One of these days I'm going to save the contents of a crop to use as stuffing when the bird is roasted. But so far, I've not progressed that far down the road of gourmet extremism.

Care in the Field

Field dressing is a very tired subject. Nearly all hunters already know the importance of promptly gutting their game and allowing the carcass to cool to preserve the natural flavors. I will spare us all a lecture and, in its place, pass along a few tips that one or another of us might not yet have put to use.

One of them involves the use of a gut hook, as was described in chapter 5. This little implement, whether it be part of a fancy folding knife or merely a bent length of coat hanger wire (or even a notched twig), permits the hunter to remove all of a gamebird's intestines through the anus. The technique is quick and clean, and it enables a more complete dressing-down of the bird to be deferred for a few hours or so.

Many hunters sidestep gutting by pulling the breast off the bird and discarding everything else. There are several different ways to do this, and some of them don't even require the use of a knife. The grouse, when freshly killed, is an easily cleaned bird; the skin slips away from the carcass and the various parts can be separated from each other with a few deft twists and tugs. Still, the job leaves hands sticky and, if a plastic bag has been forgotten, presents the problem of what to do with the bare carcass. It's literally impossible to wash away all the bits of dry leaves and other debris that attach to a skinned carcass as soon as it's tucked away in a gamebag.

Meat cleanliness is every bit as important as gutting and cooling for avoiding a "tainted" taste. I usually just apply the gut hook and then go right back to hunting. (After all, where one grouse was lurking, there's apt to be another nearby.) But I never place the fallen grouse in the gamebag, unless the weather is so cold that meat cooling can take place there. Most often, I hang the bird from my belt by tucking its head between the belt and my hip. There are waist-belt game carriers on the market which serve this same purpose, but just a piece of leather thong or broken shoelace will hold the bird as securely to a standard belt. By carrying a grouse this way, you expose the carcass to the cooling effects of circulating air. Anyone who has ever pulled the disheveled, damp carcass of a grouse from the stifling recesses of a gamebag knows that there must be a better way to handle food. There is: it's the belt-carry method.

Quick Fillets

Filleting is done if the grouse is to be pan-fried or used as the main ingredient in a casserole. The fillets are cut from the breast, and no further cleaning of the bird is necessary. Virtually all the white meat on a grouse can be removed as two slabs of breast muscle, one from each side of the bird. With a little practice, the filleting can be done in less than a minute. It's easy.

To remove the first fillet, plunge the knife straight into the grouse at the centerline of the breast, slightly to one side of the keel-shaped breastbone. Then slice from front to rear of the carcass, using the breastbone as a guide for the knife. Trim outwards along the underlying ribcage until the meat falls away.

Complete Dressing

Unlike filleting, a complete dressing leaves the carcass whole and pretty for roasting in traditional fashion. It matters little whether the job is done in the field or on the shelf beside the kitchen sink, except that indoor dressing usually ends with a chase across the floor after a few loose feathers float everywhere.

I don't recommend plucking, at least not for the ruffed grouse. The main idea behind leaving the skin on most gamebirds is to hold the natural fats in place during roasting. That's where the fat is on any bird—just under the skin. But the grouse doesn't have enough fat to warrant saving. Flavor and meat juiciness can be enhanced in far easier ways. Plucking can be relatively simple if the bird is first doused for less than a minute in water that is just on the verge of boiling. Any longer or hotter and the skin will cook—you'll end up skinning the bird whether you want to or not. Really, skinning is by far the best way to remove the feathers. Ironically, it is the absence of fat under a grouse's skin that makes peeling the skin off the carcass so easy.

The following seven steps for the complete dressing of a grouse can be completed within a few minutes.

1. Remove the wings. Slit the skin just forward of each "elbow" and dislocate the first joint. Cut free. There is virtually no meat on the wings, so discard them.
2. Remove the lower legs. Dislocate the first joint above the scaled leg and cut free from tendons.
3. Save the fantail. Probe the base of the tail with fingers until the triangular base where the feather shafts are embedded is found. Cut so that the base remains attached to tail feathers. After removing fantail, strip away the layer of feathers on the underside; this will expose flesh at base, which also should be removed. Set fantail aside for later preserving as a memento of the hunt.
4. Remove head and neck. Under all those feathers, a grouse's neck resembles a long pencil stuck into a potato. There's no meat on it

worth saving, so sever the neck close to the body, just behind the ruffs.

5. Skin the carcass. Simple pulling and tearing works as well as any other method. Start with the breast where the skin slips away easily. Get the legs started by pushing the "knee" inwards towards the body.

6. Clean the body cavity. Cut an opening from anus to tip of the breastbone. Reach in with finger or spoon to remove heart and liver. These are the world's most expensive giblets, so save them. Wash bird inside and out.

7. Inspect carcass for shot damage. Pellets can be removed with a nail of which the point has been hammered into a miniature scoop. Be gentle: raw grouse flesh tears very easily.

Preserving Natural Flavor and Tenderness

Because grouse flesh has such a low fat and moisture content, it is particularly susceptible to freezer burn and subsequent loss of flavor. Wrap grouse more securely than you would other meats to be frozen. Or, better yet, freeze grouse carcasses in water. Paper milk cartons in one-half gallon size are just right for encasing two grouse in ice for the long sleep until destiny brings them to the table. Freezing this way totally prevents freezer burn. And during subsequent thawing, it provides ideal conditions for tenderizing the meat. I'll explain.

Tenderness results from meat aging. Many people don't even want to hear about the "aging" of wild game, but that's because they've confused it with plain-and-simple rotting. The proper aging of meat, however, is the result of enzyme actions, not bacterial growth. These enzyme actions begin as soon as the animal is killed, and the first stage results in a stiffness of the muscle tissues called *rigor mortis*. (Bear with me; I have a point to make.) If the meat is cooked during this period of stiffness, it will be extremely tough. Later, the enzyme action will relax the muscles and additionally begin to break down the connective tissues. This is what aging really is.

Timing is essential in the correct preparation of a wild game supper. For example, a whitetail deer carcass does not go into full rigor mortis for about 24 hours, so a celebration dinner is possible (and tender) on the evening of the kill. But a grouse is a smaller and different sort of creature. Its flesh becomes temporarily tough within just a few minutes after the kill, and the relaxation period requires at least half a day before the meat is tender again. If the meat was in rigor mortis when frozen, it will still be tough when first thawed.

Dr. Tom Goodwin of the University of Arkansas (Dept. of Animal Sciences) advises that ruffed grouse and other gamebirds should be aged in water for a *minimum* of twelve hours before cooking. Longer is better. If a grouse carcass has been frozen with water in a milk carton, it can be thawed *and* aged briefly in that same container.

I have also gone the route of hanging grouse in the shade of the garage for several days of cool autumn temperatures. This more traditional method also produces good results, although some drying of the meat is apt to occur. According to convention, a hung bird should not be dressed until feathers can be plucked with no resistance. Marinating is still another means of achieving tenderness; the aging process continues while the acidic marinade is penetrating the tissues. But be sure to select a marinade that has a flavor compatible with grouse.

The World's Best Recipes for Grouse

There is no other fowl, wild or domestic, that has a flavor quite like that of ruffed grouse. Some people don't like it. There is a subtleness here that easily escapes the unappreciating palate. Like lobster, mushrooms, escargot, trout, and other recognized delicacies, grouse should be savored more for its *uniqueness* than for its similarities to more common foods.

All of the recipes selected for this book have met the standard of not masking the basic wild flavor of the ruffed grouse. I have been told, and have read a total of at least a thousand times, that grouse "should be roasted wrapped in bacon strips." I absolutely do not agree with this. Bacon or salt pork makes a grouse taste like pig meat. Could you logically expect anything else?

Grouse flavor originates in the lean tissues and then is trapped by whatever oils and juices are present during cooking. Fats, lards, and suets have overpowering flavors of their own, and the essence of grouse flavor can be destroyed if they're used. It's best to not use the fats of other animals with grouse. Instead, apply the likes of butter, vegetable oils, select sauces, and moist stuffings to capture and enhance true grouse flavor. There also are a few spices (mustard, curry, and thyme are examples) that augment the taste of wild grouse without changing it into something else.

If the bird is to be roasted or braised, best results are obtained by using the *whole* bird. That way, stuffing can be added and the heat and moisture of cooking can be properly distributed. Whole grouse should always be cooked with the breast *down*, instead of up in traditional posture, so that more intimate contact with hot, moisturizing juices is maintained.

Many recipes involving elaborate sauces work better with fillets than with the whole bird. Casseroles, on the other hand, need only small pieces of meat, which can most easily be obtained if the carcass is first lightly parboiled and then deboned. In any concoction of grouse, include the dark meat of the legs. They're a rich contribution that should not be wasted.

The following recipes begin with the easiest to prepare, and from there run the gamut from almost-easy through elaborate and time-consuming. All of them produce delicious results.

Fried Thunder

This means of cooking ruffed grouse is so simple that it hardly qualifies as a recipe. But I've included it here to make the point that a meal of grouse doesn't really need all those elaborate sauces or stuffings to qualify for gourmet status.

Grouse breast fillets and legs
Margarine
Salt and pepper

Heat the pan, melt the margarine, and fry the grouse. That's certainly not too difficult even for the beginner. Don't overcook, as this will toughen the meat and drive out natural moisture.

Some folks first lightly parboil the whole grouse carcass, bone the meat, slice the breast portions, and then brown in a frying pan. Grouse cooked this way has a better chance of remaining juicy and tender because less frying time is required.

Fried Grouse with Mushrooms

My wife Peg developed this recipe and I'm glad she did. It produces a succulent combination of interesting textures.

2 grouse (fillets and legs)
1–1½ C. oat flour
½ t. paprika or sage
½ t. salt
¼ t. pepper
⅓ C. milk
1 egg

Crisco or other shortening for frying
Mushrooms
1 T. margarine, melted

To make the oat flour, use quick or old fashioned oats, uncooked. Place oats in a blender or food processor. Blend for 60 seconds. Leave slightly coarse.

Combine oat flour with other dry ingredients and use to coat grouse pieces. Dip pieces in mixture of milk and egg. Coat again with dry ingredients. Fry in hot shortening (½ inch deep in electric fry pan set at 350°) until tender and golden brown. Turn frequently. Sauté desired amount of sliced mushrooms in melted margarine. Cook until tender.

Serve grouse with fried mushrooms, wild rice, and a spinach salad.

Poached Grouse

Contributed by Polly and Skip Woods, Jamestown, New York.

Breast fillets from 2 grouse
Recipe Basic White Sauce (p. 192)
Fresh mushrooms
Wine

Make a white sauce. Add fresh mushrooms and a little wine. Cover breasts of grouse with mushroom sauce and bake at 350° for 30 minutes.

Grouse Amandine

Contributed by Polly and Skip Woods, Jamestown, New York.

4 grouse
½ C. margarine
½ C. blanched almonds, slivered
1 t. lemon juice
4 slices bread, trimmed, fried crisp in butter

Place clean, dry birds in covered roasting pan. Roast for 30 minutes, or until tender, basting frequently with melted margarine and pan drippings. Add almonds, lemon juice, and remaining margarine and heat. Place grouse on fried bread slices. Pour almond sauce over all.

Roast Grouse in Mustard Shell

This is another Peggy Walrod original.

For each bird use ½ cup stuffing (See recipes on page 192) and 1 tablespoon mustard. (We prefer a spicy, brown mustard such as Gulden's or Dijon.) It forms a shell during cooking that seals in the moisture.

Place the prepared stuffing in the cavity of each clean, dry bird. Pull legs up and backward toward the breast of the bird. Using twine, tie the legs together and high, close to body. This keeps the stuffing inside and helps prevent the legs from drying out. Place in a small roasting pan. Using a knife, cover each bird with 1 tablespoon mustard. (Carcass must be dry or mustard won't adhere to it.) Roast uncovered for 30–45 minutes depending on the size of the bird.

Try serving with fluffy sweet potatoes for an interesting change.

Grouse – Chinese Style

Contributed by Zoe Ann and Jim Ritchie, Smicksburg, Pennsylvania.

            1–2 grouse
              1 chicken bouillon cube
             ½ C. water
              1 can cream of celery soup
              1 4-ounce can mushrooms and liquid
             ½ t. soy sauce
              1 can chop suey vegetables

Bake grouse in covered casserole in a mixture of bouillon cube and ½ cup water at 350° for about 1½ hours, or until tender. Let grouse cool for a few minutes; debone meat and cut into small pieces.

Combine remaining ingredients. Add the pieces of grouse and heat until boiling. Serve over hot fluffy rice.

Grouse in Sour Cream

Contributed by Zoe Ann and Jim Ritchie, Smicksburg, Pennsylvania.

            1–2 grouse, quartered
              1 can cream of mushroom or chicken soup
             ¼ C. Parmesan cheese
                Dash pepper, parsley
              1 4-ounce can mushrooms and liquid
             ½ C. sour cream

Combine soup, cheese, pepper, parsley, and mushrooms. Pour mixture over grouse in a casserole dish. Bake at 350° for about 1½ hours. Remove grouse. Add sour cream to soup mixture. Serve with either wild or white rice.

Grouse in Red Wine

Here's an easy and delicious way to fix grouse. It's a favorite where I live.

        2 grouse, quartered or filleted
        2 T. margarine
        2 medium onions, sliced
        ½ C. chicken broth or bouillon
        1 C. red wine
        1 T. cornstarch
        Salt and pepper to taste

Melt margarine in bottom of small roasting pan. Brown onions and grouse pieces. Add chicken broth and red wine. Cover and roast at 350° for 45 minutes to 1 hour until tender. Turn grouse occasionally so all parts are submerged in liquid. Meat surfaces will turn dark purple in color. Remove grouse. Thicken pan juices with cornstarch mixed with water. Season to taste. Serve sauce on the side with buttered noodles.

Grouse Casserole

Contributed by Debbie and Rick Sanders, Lakewood, New York.

    2–3 grouse breasts
      2 10-ounce packages frozen broccoli (chopped)
      2 cans cream of mushroom soup
      1 C. mayonnaise
      1 T. lemon juice
        Croutons that have been mixed with melted butter and
        Parmesan cheese

Cook grouse, take from bone. Cook broccoli, drain. Grease baking dish (7 x 11). Place broccoli on bottom of baking dish. Place grouse on top. Mix soup with mayonnaise and lemon juice. Pour over grouse mixture. Top with croutons. Bake at 350° for 25–30 minutes. Serves 6.

Debbie often serves the grouse with the following wild rice and sausage casserole.

     1 lb. bulk sausage
     2 medium onions, chopped
     1 4-ounce can chopped mushrooms
     1 box Uncle Ben's Wild Rice
     ½ C. flour
     ½ C. cream
     1 t. salt
     ¼ t. oregano
     ¼ t. thyme
     ¼ t. marjoram
    2½ C. chicken broth
     ½ C. slivered almonds

Sauté sausage and remove from skillet; sauté onions and mush-rooms in the fat. Cook rice according to directions. Stir flour and cream until smooth. Add seasonings and chicken broth, and cook, stirring until thick. Mix sausage, rice, onions, mushrooms, and cream sauce in shallow baking dish. Sprinkle with almonds. Bake at 350° for 30 minutes.

Bonasa au Vin

Contributed by Len Fink, Mineola, New York.

     Grouse (whole)
     Oil
     1 clove garlic
     ½ lb. whole mushrooms
     8 small whole white onions
     2 T. flour
     1 t. salt
     ¼ t. thyme
     ¼ t. pepper
     1 C. chicken broth
     2 C. dry wine or sherry
     8 small new potatoes

Skin bird. Brown in oil; remove from pan. Brown up a mixture of garlic, mushrooms, and onions. After browning remove this mixture.

Mix up the "sauce": flour, salt, thyme, and pepper. Cook for 5 minutes, making sure there's a little oil left in pan before cooking. This should result in a paste-like sauce mixture.

Put the grouse, garlic, mushrooms, and onions back into the pot along with the sauce. Add the chicken broth and wine (or sherry). Cover and simmer for about 1 hour. Add the potatoes and continue to simmer another 45–50 minutes. Remove mushrooms, onions, and potatoes. Thicken sauce with a little flour mixed with cold water. Cook for 3–5 minutes. Remove the bird and serve with the sauce.

Highland Grouse

Contributed by Bill Irvine, Cadillac, Michigan.

    2 grouse, split lengthwise
    4 T. butter
    ⅓ C. chopped onions
    ⅓ C. chopped celery
    1 clove garlic
    ½ t. thyme
    ¼ t. marjoram
      Salt and pepper to taste
    1 small box wheat pilaf
    1 C. chicken bouillon
    1 C. Half & Half
    ¼ C. raisins or slivered almonds (optional)

Rinse and dry grouse halves. Melt the butter in a large, heavy skillet and brown the grouse. Remove the grouse to a plate and keep warm. Add the onions, celery, and garlic to the remaining butter in the skillet and cook until tender (about 5 minutes). Add the spices to this mixture.

Cook the pilaf as per instructions on the box, only until the moisture is absorbed. Place the pilaf in the bottom of a Dutch oven, deep casserole, or deep skillet. Arrange the grouse breast-up over the pilaf. Mix the bouillon and Half & Half together and pour over the grouse and pilaf. Sprinkle the raisins or almonds over the grouse. Cover and bake at 350° for 30 minutes. Uncover and bake another 10–15 minutes to brown. Serves 4. (Alternative: Use a brown/wild rice mix instead of the pilaf.)

Braised Grouse

Braising is particularly suited to grouse because it retains all the natural juices.

> Quartered grouse
> Butter or margarine
> 2 onions, sliced
> 2 stalks celery, sliced
> 20 mushrooms, sliced
> ½ t. sage
> 1 bay leaf
> Salt and pepper to taste
> 2 C. chicken stock or bouillon
> ¾ C. canned tomatoes
> 1 t. lemon juice
> 6 pork sausages (optional)

Brown the meat first in butter or margarine. Place in a large casserole or skillet. Add remaining ingredients and cover pan tightly. Cook at simmering temperature (185°) until meat is done on range top or slow oven, approximately 1½ hours. Serve with fluffy white rice and crisp green salad.

Curried Grouse

The pungent and complex flavor of curry intermingles very nicely with the taste of wild grouse. I credit my wife with this important discovery.

> 1–2 grouse
> 2 T. margarine
> 1½ C. finely chopped, pared apple
> ½ C. chopped onion
> 1 clove garlic, chopped, or garlic powder
> 2 T. flour
> 2–3 t. curry powder
> 1 t. salt
> 2 C. milk

Boil grouse until tender, 45 minutes to an hour. Bone and cut meat into cubes. Melt margarine; add apples, onions, and garlic. Cook for 5 minutes. Stir in flour, curry powder, and salt. Slowly blend in milk. Cook and stir until thick. Add grouse. Serve over hot, cooked rice with crisp green beans and a mandarin orange jello salad.

Grouse Breasts with Raisin Sauce

This is a favorite recipe at our house. The flavor of the raisin sauce blends well with ruffed grouse.

2 grouse fillets
2 T. margarine

Brown grouse in melted margarine in heavy frying pan. Add 1 cup water. Cover and cook until tender, approximately 45 minutes. Remove to serving platter. Serve with wild rice and 1 recipe Raisin Sauce. (Recipe follows.)

Raisin Sauce

Originally from Bob and Betty Foster, Charleston, West Virginia.

½ C. brown sugar
1 t. mustard (use Gulden's Prepared)
1 T. flour

Mix and add:
1½ t. vinegar
2 T. lemon juice
1½ C. water
⅓ C. seedless raisins

Cook over low heat until thick, stirring constantly. Makes 1¾ cups.

Orange Sauce

2 T. margarine
3 T. flour
1 C. hot bouillon
½ C. orange juice
1 T. orange peel
1 t. lemon peel
1 t. sherry (optional)
Pinch of cayenne

Melt margarine in saucepan. Blend in flour. Add bouillon, and stir over medium heat until thickened. Add remaining ingredients and mix well. Makes 1½ cups.

Basic White Sauce

½ C. margarine
3 T. flour
2 C. milk

Melt margarine. Stir in flour. Add milk, stirring until thickened. Makes 2 cups.

Simple Wine Marinade

1 C. red or white wine
¼ C. vinegar
¼ C. water
½ t. salt
¼ t. pepper
1 medium onion, sliced

The tiny body cavity of a ruffed grouse may not seem to warrant the effort of preparing a stuffing, but stuffing provides tasty moisture while the bird is cooking. An extra portion can be cooked as a side dish to stuff the hunter.

Apple-Celery-Onion Stuffing

Herb-flavored croutons
Butter and water (according to directions with croutons)
1 chopped apple, including skin
2 stalks celery, chopped
1 small onion, chopped

Make amount of stuffing desired, following recipe on crouton box. Add apple, onion, and celery. Mix together. Stuff birds. Place extra stuffing in a greased casserole and bake for 30 minutes. Makes 4 cups.

Cranberry-Apple Stuffing

2½ C. cooked long grain or wild rice
1 C. chopped celery
2 C. chopped apples
2 C. fresh cranberries, cut in half

Mix all ingredients. Stuff grouse. Bake any remainder in a greased casserole for 30 minutes.